Will the Real
Jack the Ripper

Arthur Douglas

[Spitalfields Market.]

Published by Countryside Publications Limited, School Lane, Brinscall, Chorley, Lancashire.

Text© Arthur Douglas, 1979.

Printed by Tamley-Reed Limited.

ISBN 0 86157 025 1

Contents

Will the Real Jack the Ripper is illustrated in line and tone, with map sections and a composite map included. There is a bibliography and a list of specialist book shops.

Episode One: Shadows Before

From the first Ripper murder – that on the thirty-first day of August in the year eighteen-hundred and eighty-eight – to the last – that on the ninth day of November in the same year – the span of time was ten weeks and a day, and the number of victims, if one includes the Berner Street body, just five.

On this reckoning, the scourge of Whitechapel, as Jack the Ripper came to be regarded, was not a mass murderer as were, for example, France's Henri Désiré Landru, otherwise known as "Bluebeard", or, more recently, Albert DeSalvo, alias the Boston Strangler, nor yet the Monster of Dusseldorf, Peter Kürten, and there are those who, either because they are disappointed with the Ripper's tally or because they genuinely feel that his score was greater than five, seek to extend his list of conquests.

As a consequence, a number of such candidates make their appearance in Ripper and Ripper-associated literature, and can be divided into what may be termed pre-August and post-November categories. Ex-Detective Sergeant Leeson, for instance, writing in his autobiographical *Lost London* of the Frances Coles murder during the winter of eighteen-hundred and ninety-one, left himself no room for doubt . . . *the poor mutilated body was taken to the station, and soon Dr. Phillips . . . was examining another fearful example of the work of the man the police could not catch, for the revolting nature of the woman's injuries left no doubt as to the author of the crime.*

In no doubt either was Sir Melville MacNaghten, who joined Scotland Yard as an Assistant Chief Constable in the year immediately following the Ripper's rampage, and who wrote in his official notes . . . *now the Whitechapel Murderer had five victims and five victims only*, and who then went on to name those we shall become familiar with in this present reconstruction.

There are some, also, who would find significance in the dates of and the intervals between the murders, as if each act were a blood-red bead on an astral abacus, and Dr. Forbes Winslow, in particular, was to arrive at an intricate lunar rhythm theory to accommodate the spring and neap of events. But just as the numbers game stops, officially, as five, so, for most of us, are the Ripper's depredations proscribed not so much by the scatter of the heavens as by the more earthly logistics of time, place and opportunity.

If, then, Jack the Ripper's undoubted grip on the then public mind cannot be attributed to what, in modern industrial language, might be called his productivity, and may be only partially accounted for by the contemptuous sadism of his technique, from whence sprang his enduring, if diabolical, charisma?

The imperfect answer is to cast the East End of London, and essentially that slum within a slum known as Whitechapel, as a malignant, concience-pricking growth festering within the body corporate of Victorian society, and to contrast the degradation of its indigenous poor and the squalor in which they dragged out an existence with the pampered lives of the prating middle-class do-gooders who derived the substance of their well-being from the exploitation of those they sought to patronize.

This – the innermost core of London's East End, with its plexus of mean, evil streets and courts, its teeming tenements, its almost contiguous brothels, gin shops and doss houses, its rookeries and its vermin-infested slaughter-houses, where the spillage from pole-axed beasts ran more freely than did the water from the communal taps that served the surrounding dwellings – this was the stage that awaited someone like Jack the Ripper.

From the moment he made his bow, Jack played his part with consumate artistry, and to an ever growing audience, which, though rabid in its increasing fear and loathing, never doubted his virtuosity, for, above all else, he was the man who removed the coverings from the legs of the Victorian's tables and chairs; he was, moreover, the one man in all England who, by his deeds, called a whore a whore and not a fallen angel, and who, by eviscerating his victims proclaimed that the bellies of the poor were just as empty.

In choosing to emerge from his well-oiled trap-doors as and when he did, Jack the Ripper fluxed his unique talent with rare timing; the workless very poor were becoming restless, the reforming, not to say revolutionary, zeal of crusading Socialism was disturbing the *status quo*; already there had been riots and near riots, and if the Ripper's actions should cause these subversive elements to polarize, then the survival of the State itself – the monarchy, even – might be at risk.

Such was the climate of the times and the backdrop against which Jack the Ripper played his part, a part that was to cast him as *Merlin the Magician*, the *Demon King* and *Nemesis* all rolled into one, and in which guise he would, throughout that long autumn of eighteen-hundred and eighty-eight, hold more than the harlots of Whitechapel on a knife-edge of dread.

Episode Two: Early One Mourning

It is approximately 3.15 a.m. on Friday, the thirty-first day of August, in the year eighteen-hundred and eighty-eight, and Police Constable 97-J John Neil passes uneventfully through the ill-lit length of Bucks Row in London's East End.

Half-an-hour later, at approximately 3.45 a.m., he re-enters the street and part way along it shines his lantern on the body of a woman lying supine at the gated entrance to some stables. The woman's wide-open eyes, her generally dishevelled appearance and the smell of gin about her persuade the constable that she is drunk, and it is not until he bends to lift her that he perceives otherwise.

Attracting the attention of another policeman, Neil sends him for medical assistance, and soon, at approximately 4.00 a.m., Dr. Ralph Llewellyn, who lives in nearby Whitechapel Road, arrives on the scene. The doctor's examination, made in the light of police lanterns, is perfunctory: he ascertains that the throat has been cut from side to side, with the carotid arteries severed; that there is a little blood in the gutter near the throat wound; and that the victim's extremities are not yet cold.

This done, Dr. Llewellyn orders the body removed to the mortuary and, without waiting to oversee his instructions, returns to his bed. It is not yet 5 a.m.

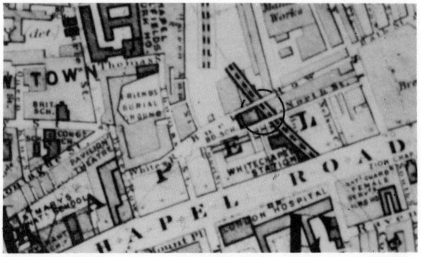

Bucks Row, later Durward Street (Stanford's Map of London). By courtesy City of London Guildhall Library.

Mary Ann (Polly) Nichols – for that was who the murdered woman proved to be – was a worn-out prostitute in her early forties who was seen last alive, though very drunk, by her friend Emily Holland, at the corner of Osborn Street and Whitechapel Road. According to Holland, Polly Nichols was intent upon earning the price of a doss-house bed in Flower and Dean Street when she set off along the Whitechapel Road that fateful Friday morning.

About one hour later – and certainly between 3.15 a.m. and 3.45 a.m., when Constable Neil's beat took him past the same spot in Bucks Row – Polly Nichols was dead, her new straw bonnet (portentously trimmed with black velvet), to which she had alluded when taking a tipsy leave of Emily Holland, lying pathetically at her side.

The time element was honed tantalizingly finer by the fact that between P.C. Neil's visits, two Spitalfields porters – George Cross and John Paul – had also come upon Nichols, and, following some debate as to her condition, had continued as far as Bakers Row, where they reported the incident to a patrolling constable.

Cross, almost immediately followed by Paul, entered Bucks Row at — what time? Leonard Matters, writing in the first definitive work on the subject, *The Mystery of Jack the Ripper*, first published in 1929, gives the time as 3.45 a.m. Tom Cullen, in *The Crimes and Times of Jack the Ripper*, originally published as *Autumn of Terror*, hazards 3.20 a.m., while Robin Odell, in *Jack the Ripper in Fact and Fiction*, agrees with Matters. Daniel Farson, in his book titled simply *Jack the Ripper*, is not specific, but implies by subtraction that it was minutes before 3.45 a.m. And Donald Rumbelow, reconstructing events in *The Complete Jack the Ripper*, opts for "shortly before 4 o'clock", and does not define P.C. Neil's times of arrival at all. It is left to Stephen Knight, in *Jack the Ripper: The Final Solution*, to quote verbatim from contemporary police reports and fix Neil's movements and those of Cross and Paul at 3.45 a.m. and 3.40 a.m., respectively.

Given that Cullen is a little early and Rumbelow somewhat late in their estimation of the porters' time of arrival, logic has it that "things were happening in Bucks Row" soon after 3.15 a.m. We gather from Matters and Odell that P.C. Neil's beat took him there from the west, or Old Montague Street, end, and it is possible that Polly Nichols and a companion entered it together, virtually in Neil's wake. On the other hand, her killer could have been there already, trading on certain physical aspects of the place to evade the passing constable.

Bucks Row – later Durward Street – was peculiar in that what commenced as a single wide thoroughfare became, about half-way down its length, two narrow-pronged continuations, the one remaining as Bucks Row, the other changing to Winthrop Street. All ran roughly parallel to Whitechapel Road and were connected to it by various streets and passages crossing the *Metropolitan District Railway.* Contrary, therefore, to the bated-breath supposition that the killer was all but flushed by the arrival of the first of the two porters, the truth probably is that he had reasonable time between, say, 3.20 a.m. and 3.35 a.m. to do what he had to do and depart.

That Polly Nichols had departed before him, in even more dramatic terms than originally supposed, was confirmed when she was stripped and examined in the primitive mortuary shed behind the workhouse in Old Montague Street. There, at a little after 7.00 a.m., in the presence of two police inspectors, it was discovered that Nichols had been disembowelled. Whether this was done before or after her throat was cut is open to conjecture, but one would have thought the latter – if only to prevent the screams that must otherwise have alerted the slaughter-house workers who were already busy in the vicinity of Bucks Row, or reached the ears of the several patrolling policemen, not to mention those of the allegedly wide-awake Mrs. Emma Green who lived hard by.

Kitchen in a Single Women's Lodging House, Spitalfields. By courtesy City of London Guildhall Library.

As it was, they heard nothing and the manner in which Polly Nichols was conceivably silenced is deserving of attention. At the time of the *post mortem*, Dr. Llewellyn noted that there were two gashes across the neck, one above the other and each starting from the left, and that there was bruising along the lower edge of the jaw on the right-hand side of the face, with another bruise on the other side. He formed the opinion that the first mark was consistent with pressure from a thumb, and it follows that the second was the result of finger pressure. If, as the bruising suggests, Nichols was gripped by one hand and slashed by a knife held in the other, and if we accept as postulates both the direction of wounding and the interpretation of the bruising, then there is one way and one way only in which she was dispatched – by someone gripping her jaw from the front between the fingers and thumb of the right hand while cutting her throat with the left.

But only if one accepts the postulates. Read fingers for thumb in relation to the bruises and the killer changes hands and position. Actually there is merit in this latter possibility, for by crooking his arm and gripping the jaw from behind the killer would be assisted in cutting deep into his victim's neck by her own efforts to pull away from him. It would also reduce the risk of spontaneous blood-staining.

In pursuing the "back-to-front" theory, its advocates have spent time in pondering as to how Jack – and from here on we shall call him that, although he had not yet made the name indelibly his own – as to how Jack managed to get behind Nichols and lay hands upon her. The answer, surely, lies in the circumstances of the moment. It was dark; they were there – or so she must have believed – for a certain purpose, and when a suitable gateway presented itself what more natural than she should lead the way, or be manoeuvred into so doing? Furthermore, Polly Nichols was not merely unsuspecting; she was drunk.

Much thought too has been devoted to the small amount of blood present in Bucks Row – "not more than would fill two wine-glasses", according to Dr. Llewellyn – in an attempt to place the actual murder elsewhere. Donald Rumbelow, however, informs us that blood there was – and in plenty, blotted up by the woman's garments. Yet there is no mention of this at the mortuary, where a police inspector made an inventory of each item of clothing as it was removed: a rust-coloured ulster, with seven big brass buttons; a brown linsey frock; two petticoats, marked with the tell-tale legend *Lambeth Workhouse*; a pair of brown stays; black wool stockings and spring-sided boots.

There *is* mention, on the other hand, at the inquest on Nichols, of washing the body and freeing the petticoats by . . . *cutting the bands and peeling them down*. Also of a shirt-waist that was . . . *cut down the front*, as though these might have been stuck together by congealed blood. All are agreed, however, that her sole personal possessions were a comb and a piece of broken mirror.

Reportage differs sharply in the matter of names. The constable P.C. Neil hailed from Brady Street to fetch Dr. Llewellyn is either *Hain* or *Thain,* while the one to whom the two market porters hurried is sometimes *Misen* and frequently *Mizen.* The porters themselves do not escape the confusion, being termed, correctly, *George* Cross and *John* Paul for the most part, but otherwise rechristened *Charles* and *Robert* in a police report, while one Ripperologist writes of *William* Cross and has him and Paul scooting back to report to P.C. Thain in Brady Street rather than to P.C. Mizen in Bakers Row. But these contradictions are mere literary lapses, not at all the same thing as the credibility gaps through which slip so many suspects later on.

This, then, was the early morning tableau – unremarkable in itself in a day and age notorious for its brutality – that heralded a season of terror in Victorian England. The fanciful went so far as to opine that the autumnal skies were incarnadine that year, that the air folk breathed was thickened by evil. Fanciful or not, those same skies were to witness blood-letting of a kind that not even London's leprous East End knew, and that same air was to sustain Jack the Ripper as he sharpened his knife . . . and his appetite.

Episode Three: The Doctor's Dilemma

It is shortly after 6.00 a.m. on the eighth day of September, one week and a day following the murder of Polly Nichols in Bucks Row, and a posse of police, led by Inspector Joseph Chandler of Commercial Street Police Station, Spitalfields, surrounds an object lying in a yard at the rear of No. 29 Hanbury Street. It proves to be the body of Annie Chapman, *alias* Sievey, or Siffey, but best known within the purlieus of Whitechapel as Dark Annie.

As Inspector Chandler and Dr. George Bagster Phillips, the police surgeon, conduct their examination, the shadowy sockets that are tenement windows turn pale with gathering faces. But strain as they will, these silent spectators, they cannot discern what the doctor sees – that Dark Annie Chapman has been butchered in a mode and manner more savage even than was Polly Nichols.

The throat wound runs in a ragged rictus from left to right and back again, and a scarf knotted round the ravaged neck seems unequal almost to its supposed purpose of retaining the head. The body lies in a recess between some steps and the fence of the house next door, with the left arm across the breast and the legs steepled and spread, a posture which leaves no room for doubt that, like Nichols, the victim has been disembowelled. The small intestines and a flap of the abdomen wall lie across the right shoulder, still connected to the rest of the gut within the body, while two more flaps of flesh rest in their own blood across the other shoulder. The clandestine surgery is thus seen to be crude but extensive, and a specific organ is missing.

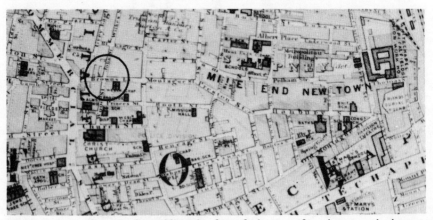

Hanbury Street, shown at the middle right of Stanford's Map of London, was also known by that name as far west as its junction with Commercial Street, and it was towards that end that No. 29 lay.

More blood, in lesser amounts, appears on the fence in the form of smears some fourteen inches from the ground and adjacent to the spillage from the throat wound, and as spots on the wall of the house some eighteen inches from the ground and diminishing in size from that of a sixpence to the head of a pin.

Whatever the motive for the outrage it is not robbery, for arranged near Dark Annie's person are certain objects, including, at her feet, a few pennies and two new farthings; also two brass rings torn from the middle finger of the left hand. Elsewhere is part of a franked envelope bearing the crest of the Sussex regiment; also two pills, while nearby, a few feet from a tap, is a leather apron soaked with water.

Whether these things – the apron and the brass rings excepted – came from the inside pocket that was slashed open when the killer lifted Annie's skirts is, however, not a matter to be too long debated in the chill of a September morning, and soon the mortal remains of Dark Annie Chapman are being transported in the same ambulance and to the same mortuary that accommodated Polly Nichols eight days before.

* * * * * *

The classic unities of time and place are perhaps nowhere brought into more fascinating, not to say crucial, juxtaposition than in the case of murder, and, this being so, in no greater degree than in the murder of Dark Annie Chapman.

An impoverished widow in her middle forties, and a known prostitute, Chapman was last placed alive, if drunk, at shortly before 2.0 a.m. by the keeper of a common lodging-house at 35 Dorset Street, when and where she admitted to being destitute of the price of a bed, adding, "I am weak and ill and have been in the infirmary".

In turning Dark Annie into the street, the lodging-house keeper just as surely turned her into a corpse, for she was destined to share the early morning chill of Whitechapel with a predator whose lust for blood had been whetted rather than assuaged by the savouring of Polly Nichols. but at what time did she die? And where?

It must have been quite 6.30 a.m. when Bagster Phillips first examined Chapman and so formed the basis of his later expressed opinion that . . . *she had then been dead for two hours, or more;* thus putting the time of death at not later than 4.30 a.m. Yet at approximately 4.45 a.m. when John Richardson, a Spitalfields porter, had loitered in the yard behind No. 29 Hanbury Street

Annie Chapman's body wasn't there. That it was there at a few minutes after 6.0 a.m. when John Davis, another porter, went into the yard, is not in dispute. Neither is there any reason to doubt the evidence of Albert Cadosh, who was passing through the yard next door when he heard a woman's voice from the far side of the fence, followed by the sound of a fall. If Cadosh thought about the incident at all, it was probably to conclude that a prostitute and her client were embroiled in some slight altercation. But it was none of his business and he moved out of earshot, the time being, in his own estimation, about 5.20 a.m.

Subsequently, Mrs. Elizabeth Long, the wife of a park-keeper, was to testify that at 5.30 a.m. she saw Annie Chapman (whom she later identified at the mortuary) talking to a man at the street end of the passage belonging to No. 29. She described the man as . . . *dark, over forty, a little taller than Chapman, and wearing a brown deer-stalker hat and* (she thought) *a dark coat. He was of "shabby genteel" appearance and looked like a foreigner.*

Mrs. Long and Cadosh came so close together that morning that a few minutes difference must have seen them exchange the time of day. Perhaps, in its most literal sense, that is what they did, in which case their testimony must surely have been regarded as chronologically conclusive were it not for Bagster Phillip's assertion, later somewhat modified, that Chapman had been dead at least two hours when he saw her at 6.30 a.m. It follows that either Richardson, Cadosh and Long were mistaken or lying, or that Phillips was wrong, *or that the murder was committed elsewhere.*

To think so is to ignore Cadosh and Long entirely and argue that the comparative lack of blood in the yard and the trail of blood leading *up* the passage from the street are otherwise inconsistent, and that the organ removed from the body – the uterus and its several appendages – was missing not because it was taken away *but because it wasn't brought.* What the premise fails to accommodate is that Chapman's clothing could have absorbed a considerable volume of blood, enough at any rate to leave a trail as the body was wheeled *down* the passage on its way to the mortuary. Tom Cullen, in his researches into the Ripper murders, actually located a witness who claimed, as a boy, to have followed the stretcher and its bloody spoor down Hanbury Street.

We return, therefore, to the more widely held, if less dramatic, view that George Bagster Phillips was wrong by not less than one hour in estimating the time of death. His critics emphasize the adverse conditions in which the examination was made, pointing out that Annie Chapman's torso was exposed – literally so in the case of her eviscerated abdomen – to the leaching touch of an autumn morning and that she was in a chronic state of physical deprivation. Taken together these factors could have induced acute *hypothermia*, thus misleading Bagster Phillips into thinking death occurred earlier than in fact it did.

That he did not thereafter conduct a *post mortem* until Saturday afternoon, after the body had been stripped and washed, goes to compound the possibility of error on his part, and it is interesting that he does not dwell in his report on either *rigor* or *hypostasis,* accepted criteria in establishing the lapse of time following death.

The ensuing confusion was compounded by the police issuing the description of a man . . . *seen entering a passage of a house at which murder was committed at 2.00 a.m.* As far as is known no such incident was reported at that time, and the description is sufficiently like that of the man seen at about 5.30 a.m. by Mrs. Long to suppose that, somehow, the one became the other.

Thus far, then, and only thus far are the unities of time and place reconciled, and it is perhaps not inappropriate at this juncture to mention two more aspects of the Chapman murder that went unresolved: some significance, ranging from the arcane to the mundane, has been attributed to the disappearance of the two brass rings and the few coppers found at Dark

Kitchen in a Common Lodging House, Spitalfields. By courtesy City of London Guildhall Library.

Annie's feet. Did the rings *really* represent the two brass pillars at the entrance to Solomon's Temple? And were the coins also bound up in Masonic ritual? If so, their placing was one thing and their taking away another, for the latter implicates someone present *after* the killing.

Or were the rings stolen because they looked like gold, and the money because it was what it was? And the uterus – was that twice removed, once from its owner and once from her very proximity, as part and parcel of some as yet to be played out oedipidean compulsion? Or was it snatched up by some half-starved alley cat?

Other questions produced more positive, if disappointing, answers; the envelope found near Chapman's body was seen in her possession before she left Dorset Street, and was probably used to protect the pills dispensed at the infirmary, while the leather apron found near the water tap belonged to John Richardson, the Spitalfields porter. It is relevant to add that police inquiries of the most stringent kind left no vestige of suspicion attaching to Richardson, or to Davis and Cadosh.

The inquest on Dark Annie Chapman was opened at the *Working Lads' Institute* in Whitechapel Road on Monday, the tenth day of September, and mirrored that on Polly Nichols in that both fell within the bailiwick of Coroner Wynne E. Baxter and reached a broad measure of agreement in three related respects – the nature of the weapon, the method of immobilizing the victim and the expertise of the killer.

Dr. Ralph Llewellyn thought the knife was . . . *more likely a pointed one sith a stout back, such as a cork-cutter's or a shoe-maker's*; Dr. George Bagster Phillips visualised the weapon as being . . . *a very sharp knife, with a narrow blade some eight inches long*. Both doctors agreed that the facial bruising was consistent with the killer gripping the victim's face with one hand while the other made play with the knife. In more equivocal terms they conceded that the evisceration of the abdomen indicated some anatomical knowledge, and Bagster Phillips thought that the Chapman episode could not have been concluded in . . . *under a quarter of an hour.*

Even so, unheard and unseen by the sixteen occupants of No. 29 Hanbury Street and the numerous other folk who slept light and rose early in the dwellings near by, the Ripper did his work and departed, leaving behind not only a savagely gutted corpse but a declaration of intent so potent that its message spread like a virus. If the Nichols murder had caused the whores of Whitechapel to shiver, the manner of Annie Chapman's going reduced them to a state of abject terror. And with good reason, for soon their most morbid apprehensions would be fully realised.

Episode Four: Unfinished Business (?)

It is just 1.00 a.m. on Sunday, the thirtieth day of September, and Louis Diemschutz, weary from a day's trading in his cheap wares, costume jewellery, trinkets and the like, lets his pony find its own way between the open gates leading off Berner Street into Dutfield's Yard.

All at once, the animal baulks and Diemschutz, the adrenalin of sudden fright bringing him wide awake, dismounts from the cart and stumbles into the body of a woman lying across the carriage-way. Fetching help from the *International Workmen's Educational Club,* which occupies one side of the yard, and of which he is part-time steward, Diemschutz examines the woman in the light cast by the club windows and the flickering flame of a candle.

She is lying on her left side, with her legs drawn up and her feet against the right-hand wall. A trickle of blood runs from a wound in her neck and swells the great pool already formed on the wet ground. Hesitantly, Diemschutz reaches out and touches the body, the flesh of which is still warm. What he cannot comprehend is that if he has interrupted the ungorged Ripper at table, he has loosed on London a ravening monster.

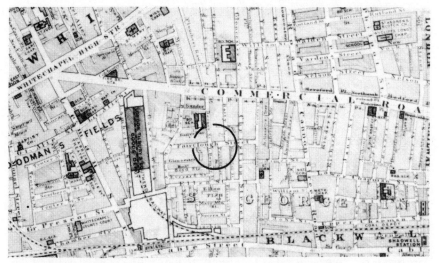

Berner Street and its junction with Fairclough Street (Stanford's Map of London). By courtesy City of London Guildhall Library.

17

Dr. Frederick Blackwell, who was the first medical man on the scene and who arrived there at approximately 1.15 a.m., had no hesitation in stating that death took place between twenty and thirty minutes earlier. This forthright opinion, corroborating as it did the general feeling that the Ripper had been disturbed by Diemschutz's arrival at 1.00 a.m., might be regarded as conclusive were it not for an almost throw-away sentence in Cullen's book that reads, "Her clothes were wet, but when they moved the body the police noticed that the ground beneath it was quite dry".

If this was so, and if, as other evidence suggests, it started to rain soon after midnight, then the Bagster Phillips syndrome is reversed and the whole time structure of the Berner Street murder collapses like a house of cards. On the other hand, several witnesses going to or coming from the club in Dutfield's Yard were ready to swear that there was no impediment to their occasions between 12.30 a.m. and 12.45 a.m., and we must conclude that the reference to dry ground is misleading.

In his book *Jack the Ripper: A New Theory*, William Stewart removed the Berner Street victim from the Ripper's repertoire because, in Stewart's understanding of the case, the throat had been cut from right to left, whereas it was the Ripper's *modus operandi* to cut in the opposite direction. Actually Stewart was wrong, and it was Dr. Blackwell's finding – and later that of Dr. George Bagster Phillips – that the throat of the woman found in Dutfield's Yard had been opened in a single sweep . . . *from left to right, partially severing the left carotid artery and completely cutting through the windpipe.*

Blackwell also ventured the opinion that she was probably pulled backwards by her scarf, but could not say whether her throat was cut while she was standing up or lying down. He was influenced, no doubt, by the finger marks – presumably bruises – across the front of each shoulder, as if she had been held thus and forced onto the ground. There is no reason, however, why these pressure marks should be so regarded; after all, women like this led promiscuous, violent lives and the legacy of some previous encounter, amorous or otherwise, could still have been evident.

Be that as it may, and with or without Cullen, it is possible that in dismissing the Berner Street interlude from its accustomed place in the sexually-inspired Ripper fugue, Stewart might have been right, if for the wrong reason. Apart from the Ripper-like neck wound, there is no evidence, indubitably, to associate this victim with his particular handiwork, and it is a matter of fact that Berner Street was well below the Aldgate–Whitechapel Road thoroughfare that seems to have acted as a southerly demarcation line as far as the other Ripper atrocities went. Certainly, then, a question mark at least must be placed against her name.

She was in fact Elizabeth – Long Liz – Stride, neé Gustaáfsdotter, born in Gottenberg, Sweden, in the year eighteen-hundred and forty-three. Long Liz, so-called because of her rawboned height, had something of a reputation as a hard-drinking, fanciful liar, which latter attribute might, just might, indicate that she was known personally by one of the suspects we shall examine later on.

When she was found, Long Liz, according to *The Times* newspaper, was clutching in her left hand a packet of cachous, and in her right hand a bunch of grapes. In due course this unlikely bunch of fruit was to reappear in one of the most ingenious Hunt-the-Ripper theories since Leonard Matters fathered the *genre* in the late 1920s. But how she came by it is only one of the mysteries surrounding Stride's movements and the company she kept in the hour before the clock of St. Mary's Whitechapel struck one on that last day in September.

Dutfield's Yard, leading off Berner Street.

19

There were three generally accepted sightings: that by William Marshall, a labourer of 64 Berner Street; that by Police Constable 452-H William Smith; and that by James Brown, a local boxmaker. According to Cullen, Marshall saw Stride at 11.45 a.m. three doors away from where he lived, with . . . *a middle-aged, clean-shaven man, about five feet six inches tall and rather stout. He was wearing* (Marshall thought) *a black cut-away coat and gloves. He was decently dressed and looked like a clerk of some sort, with an educated, mild way of speaking,* this last becoming apparent when Marshall heard him say to Stride, "You would say anything but your prayers". Whether this remark was just so much banter, or whether he knew Stride well and was alluding to her habitual loose way of talking, is a moot point.

Police Constable Smith, Cullen's second witness, reported that he was proceeding down Berner Street at about 12.35 a.m., when he observed Stride talking to . . . *a clean-shaven man of medium height, aged twenty-eight. He was of respectable appearance, and was wearing a dark overcoat, hard deer-stalker felt hat, and was holding a parcel about eighteen inches long wrapped in newspaper.*

James Brown's version was that he saw Stride at 12.45 a.m., at the corner of Fairclough Street and Berner Street, where she was talking to a man . . . *of stoutish build, about five feet seven inches tall, wearing a coat down to his heels.* He heard Stride say, "No, not tonight, some other time".

Donald Rumbelow tells us that Marshall's suspect was *not* wearing gloves, that he had on dark trousers and that he affected a round cap with a small peak to it. To P.C. Smith's description he adds that the man had dark trousers, that the parcel was about eighteen inches long by about six to eight inches wide, and that the woman had a flower in her jacket; there is no mention of the man's build.

There is confusion also concerning the ages of Marshall's and Smith's suspects, several writers saying that there was agreement between the two witnesses that the man was middle-aged. Odell makes matters worse by timing Marshall's sighting at 12.45 a.m., one hour later than the time specified by most others. He does, however, add a nice touch to the policeman's evidence in modifying the flower in Stride's jacket to maidenhair fern.

He also produces a Mrs. Mortimer – only four doors away from the murder spot – who, at between 12.30 a.m. and 1.00 a.m., alleged that she was at her street entrance when she heard a stifled cry, then a bump. Shortly after, she saw . . . *a young man carrying a shiny black bag walk quickly down the street.* Like Rumbelow, Odell expresses the view that Marshall and Smith were in agreement that their suspect was middle-aged !

Stephen Knight is diligent in finding a fifth witness, one whose deposition appears in the Home Office file, but who was not called by Coroner Baxter at the inquest. According to Knight, Israel Schwartz was in the vicinity of Dutfield's Yard at 12.45 a.m. when he saw a man stop and speak to a woman who was standing in the gateway. He tried to pull her into the street, then threw her down, saying, either for the benefit of Schwartz or a second man standing across the way, "Lipski", a derogatory term applied to Jews.

This first man was . . . *about thirty years of age, five feet five inches tall, of fair complexion, with dark hair and a small brown moustache. He was wearing a dark jacket and trousers and a black cap with a peak. He was broad shouldered and had nothing in his hands.* And the second . . . *was older and taller – about thirty-five and five feet eleven inches – with a fresh complexion, light brown hair and moustache, and was wearing a dark overcoat, a black felt hat with a wide brim, and had a clay pipe in his hand.*

There is, therefore, no shortage of witnesses but a plethora, and with one thing in common – the ability not only to see in the drizzle but to appreciate detail . . . *clean-shaven . . . of fair complexion . . . a light brown moustache . . . wearing gloves . . . not wearing gloves.* No wonder the police made the best of a bad job and issued *two* descriptions, the first based substantially on P.C. Smith's sighting, and the other owing more to Schwartz than it did to Marshall.

Schwartz is thus rendered credible, and is, paradoxically, made even more so by Brown, who said he saw Stride with a man at the corner of Fairclough Street at 11.45 a.m., the precise time that Schwartz watched her being manhandled at the entrance to Dutfield's Yard. Shift the variables by only a few minutes and it is feasible that Brown and Schwartz saw one and the same person, the quarrel witnessed by Schwartz being the aftermath of Stride's remark, "No, not tonight, some other time".

Not content with springing one surprise, Knight reveals the strange case of Matthew Packer, a fruiterer in a small way of business at 44 Berner Street, and the suppression by the police of vital evidence. It seems that on the fourth day of October, Police Sergeant Stephen White questioned Packer at the Cable Street mortuary where Stride's body lay, and where Packer now was with two men. Packer said he had been taken there to identify Stride's body, which he had since done, adding that he believed . . . *she bought some grapes at his shop at about 12 o'clock on Saturday night.*

The two men said they were private detectives, but refused, positively, to identify themselves, and persuaded Packer to leave in their company. Later, when White was at Packer's shop, the pair appeared again, this time in a hansom, and took Packer off, apparently to see Sir Charles Warren, the then Metropolitan Commissioner of Police. That such an interview took place is substantiated by the fact that Packer's statement, taken in Warren's own hand, appears in a Scotland Yard file. Another document, this time written by Chief Inspector Swanson, alludes to what can only be the same two men when it records that, following the early flurry of police activity in Dutfield's Yard, *two private enquiry men, upon searching a drain in the yard, found a grape stem which was amongst the other matter swept from the yard after its examination by the police.*

Which, in turn, leads us to the unfortunate Dr. George Bagster Phillips, who, according to Knight, played down the whole subject of the grapes at the inquest on Stride by saying, "I am convinced that the deceased had not swallowed either skin or seed of a grape within many hours of her death", and who, again according to Knight, was involved in a police conspiracy at the highest level to pervert the course of justice. Poor Bagster Phillips! Could it be that there were no grapes in Stride's stomach for the very good reason that she hadn't eaten any? And that, though Stephen Knight was right concerning the suppression of evidence and the possible employment by Warren of supra-departmental agents, the explanation was not at all sinister.

But the matter of the dead woman's clinging to the vine must await its turn, for it is first necessary to contend with yet another murder, this time in Mitre Square, which, although in the City of London, was, in a manner of speaking, only a "Stride" away.

Episode Five: Terror in Tandem

It is yet Sunday, the thirtieth day of September, and at 1.30 a.m. Police Constable 881 Edward Watkins of the City of London Police directs the beam of his lantern into the farthermost recesses of Mitre Square. Satisfied that all is as it should be, he resumes his beat, returning at 1.45 a.m. This time, in the south-western corner of the square, at the entrance to a passage leading to the backs of some empty houses, the constable's questing light shines on the body of a woman. Her posture and condition are at once significant, for it is apparent to Watkins, and to the watchman he hastily summons from a nearby warehouse, that she has been foully used.

Soon Mitre Square is seething with activity as police and officials, led by Major Henry Smith, Acting Police Commissioner for the City of London, conduct their investigation. Leaving Doctors Frederick Gordon Brown, the City Police Surgeon, and George William Sequerira to make their gross examination and then dispatch the body to the City Mortuary in Golden Lane, Major Smith loses no time in deploying his men, not hesitating to send them across City limits into the Metropolitan Police District.

There, penetrating beyond Houndsditch and Middlesex Street as far as Goulston Street, Smith's men find, in unsavoury Dorset Street, evidence that the fleeing Ripper has washed himself at a public sink. A little later, at approximately 2.55 a.m., Police Constable Long, attached to Whitechapel's H-Division, chances on a blood -stained piece of cloth lying in a passage giving onto some flats in Goulston Street, while on the dark dado of the passage is chalked a message so evocative that Sir Charles Warren himself orders it expunged.

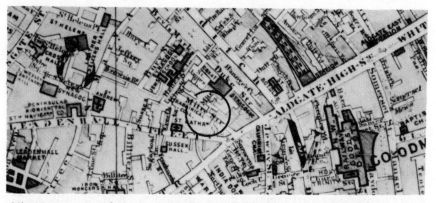

Mitre Square, City of London (Stanford's Map of London). By courtesy City of London Guildhall Library.

23

The two pawn tickets that led to the eventual identification of the Mitre Square victim as Catherine Eddowes, also known as Kate Kelly, or Conway, a forty-three year old drab living in and out of a doss-house in Fashion Street, were like flags signalling the end of a life that could be redeemed from the squalor into which it had sunk only by the pledge of the Ripper's knife.

That he weilded it well became patent when, at the inquest commenced in Golden Lane on the fourth day of October before Coroner S. F. Langham and Mr. Crawford, the City of London Solicitor, a concensus report of the several doctors involved revealed that . . . *the throat was cut across,* and that the cause of death was . . . *haemorrhage from the left carotid artery.* The subsequent mutilations amounted to . . . *a gash running from the bridge of the nose to the base of the right cheek, the nicking downwards of both lower eyelids, the partial severance of the right ear lobe, and sundry nicks and cuts about the cheeks and chin.* There was, additionally, some damage to the right eye and superficial abrasions on each side of the face.

As to the body, the mutilations were extensive, with . . . *the walls of the abdomen abducted and the intestines drawn and draped across the right shoulder.* There was . . . *considerable incidental damage, much of it caused by the removal of the left kidney and the uterus.* There had also been a good deal of blood in Mitre Square, but the doctors were of the opinion that the killer need not have come into contact with overmuch of it.

They were less than unanimous, however, concerning the degree of skill exhibited by their *alfresco* surgeon, but, bearing in mind that there were no less than four medical men, including the ubiquitous George Bagster Phillips, being canvassed for their opinion, this is perhaps not surprising. But to say, as one writer does, that three of the doctors were satisfied that the Ripper had demonstrated no more anatomical knowledge than . . . *that which could be expected of a professional butcher or meat cutter* is misleading, for Dr. Frederick Gordon Brown — who was, after all, the official City of London Police Surgeon — only surrendered to that viewpoint in response to a leading question from the City Solicitor. Indeed, earlier in his evidence, Brown had spoken of . . . *a good deal of knowledge as to the position of the organs in the abdominal cavity and the way of removing them.*

In reconstructing the murder, there are those who aver that the courses of Catherine Eddowes and Jack the Ripper were destined to polarize, that the runes of fate were cast from the coincidental moment when she was released from the cells of Bishopsgate Police Station – it being the practice of the City Police to discharge their sobering drunks in this way – and he, disturbed by the arrival of Diemschutz's pony and cart, was quitting the vicinity of Berner Street.

POLICE NOTICE.

TO THE OCCUPIER.

On the mornings of Friday, 31st August, Saturday 8th, and Sunday, 30th September, 1888, Women were murdered in or near Whitechapel, supposed by some one residing in the immediate neighbourhood. Should you know of any person to whom suspicion is attached, you are earnestly requested to communicate at once with the nearest Police Station.

Metropolitan Police Office,
30th September, 1888.

Facsimile of a police notice circularised to householders in the East End.

In fact, only the first part of the equation stands the test of proof, for whether, as Eddowes was wandering dejectedly towards that plexus of streets touching on Mitre Square, the Ripper was thrusting westwards along Commercial Road, in a state of psychological *coitus interruptus*, is one of the great imponderables of Ripperology. If he was, the ten minutes or so that it took him to reach Mitre Square would have left him sufficient time to explore the area and await, with avid yet wary eyes, the approach of his unsuspecting victim.

The time-table for the actual murder and its attendant mutilations, however, hinged, not on the Ripper's real or supposed itinerary, but on that of Eddowes and P.C. Watkins. If, as is fairly certain, Eddowes left the police station at approximately 1.00 a.m., and came down Bishopsgate Street and Houndsditch to Mitre Square, it would take her – given an aimless and still fuddled state of mind – up to twenty-five minutes to get there, that is to say a few minutes before Watkins passed through the place at 1.30 a.m.

It surely follows that, unless Eddowes and the Ripper were already lurking in the shadows or in the empty property fronting onto Mitre Street, the pair entered Mitre Square by one of its three lawful means of ingress within moments of the policeman's departure. The doctors – those same experts who would have deemed it reasonable to do in half an hour what Jack accomplished in much less – saw nothing incongruous in allocating him from three to five minutes for his grisly task. Even so, he could not long have concluded it and gone on his way before P.C. Watkins returned at 1.45 a.m.

Donald Rumbelow's theory that the Ripper and his victim were probably in one of the empty houses, where Eddowes was strangled into submission, creates more problems than it solves, in that while there was no more time, overall, available, there would be the additional hazard and delay involved in dragging Eddowes into the square proper and commencing operations in earnest.

Strangulation as a means of murder is not uncommon and the indications of such means are, therefore, unlikely to be overlooked by an experienced doctor. It is, however, argued that in the Ripper cases the mutilations to the neck could have masked the condition, but before this explanation is too readily accepted it should be understood that *post mortem hypostasis* (the discoloration, or lividity, brought about by the sinking of the blood in the lowest vessels in the body) is, according to Sir Sydney Smith,* writing in his book *Mostly Murder, well marked in asphyxia, but less so in death from bleeding*. As none of the medical reports in the Ripper case draw this distinction, the possibility of strangulation must be treated with reserve.

The likelihood of Eddowes being killed and butchered out of context with Mitre Square entirely and then dumped there seems, in the light of

* Sir Sydney Smith, C.B.E., LL.D., M.D.(Edin.), F.R.C.P. (Edin.).

information made specific in Professor Francis E. Camps' book, *Camps on Crime*, even more remote. In it Camps writes . . . *thanks to the detective work of my assistant, Sam Hardy, who discovered in the basement of the London Hospital, not only the plan* . . . *but some pencil sketches made by the doctor at the scene, we now have an accurate record of the exact nature of the wounds and the position of the surrounding objects.*

And what Dr. Frederick Brown's handiwork shows very clearly is that on either side of Eddowes' neck and shoulders, ballooning outwards like water-wings, are two substantial pools of blood. However tempting it may be in the never-ending search for a new solution to the Ripper enigma to locate the Eddowes killing other than in Mitre Square, the Camps-Brown data dictates otherwise.

From Mitre Square, then, to Dorset Street, where, according to Cullen, Major Smith's men were so hot on the trail that . . . *not quite all of the bloodstained water had gurgled down the drain* when they arrived at the public sink in which the fugitive Ripper had washed his hands. Blood-stained or not, to say that the liquid matched Jack's escape with its own sounds just too good to be true. What is true is that from Dorset Street, the police – City and Metropolitan officers alike – found themselves back-tracking to Goulston Street, where a gory scrap of rag had been dropped, like a satirical punctuation mark, beneath some writing on a wall.

This piece of cloth – later found to have been hacked from the top of the dead woman's apron – was blood-stained, and the popular notion is that a fastidious Ripper used it to wipe clean his knife. If so, why wait until he reached Goulson Street? In fact, why wait at all, when he could quite easily have wiped the blade clean where Eddowes lay? A more satisfactory explanation may be that, elated to the point of recklessness, the Ripper indulged in a mad game of catch-me-if-you-can, even to the extent of depositing tangible clues . . . the fragment of cloth . . . the water in the sink, and, possibly . . . the writing on the wall.

This writing, which appeared just within the entrance to Wentworth Dwellings in Goulston Street has been quoted variously as . . . *The Juwes* (sic) *are* not *the men that will be blamed for nothing*, and . . . *The Juwes* (sic) *are the men that will* not *be blamed for nothing*, and occupied several lines of writing; Stephen Knight suggests five. The outstanding question it poses is – did the Ripper write it? If he did not, was the clue cast there indiscriminately, possibly as the Ripper hurried past or dodged inside to avoid a passer-by? Or did he place it there knowing already that the writing existed?

The answer to the first question must incline acutely towards no. With Major Smith's men so close behind, not even saucy Jack could have found the time and nerve to dwell – not pause – sufficiently long. And in the dark? There is no

saying now whether the passage to Wentworth Dwellings was illuminated, or not, but if not – and this was the year eighteen-hundred and eighty-eight – is it tenable that anyone, least of all a man courting capture, could have chalked five lines of words in even reasonable alignment?

Whatever the truth of the matter, Sir Charles Warren's response was nothing if not pragmatic, and, despite vehement protestations from the City representatives and the less outspoken reservations of his own officials, he ordered the writing washed off, unwilling even to let it remain until the growth of the infant dawn provided sufficient light by which to take photographs. Warren's action has been pondered since the day it took place, and Stephen Knight is in no doubt that the Commissioner's conduct was due to his part in an intricate Masonic cover-up designed to protect the real perpetrators of not just the Eddowes murder but that series of murders of which hers was one.

The orthodox view is that Warren's motives were otherwise inspired, that in his judgement the allusion to *Juwes* was a threat to public order, and that this postscript to the Eddowes murder conditioned his thinking later when he came to consider the Schwartz statement in the Stride case. Schwartz, it will be remembered, had employed the anti-Jewish expression *Lipski*, which, coming to Warren's notice as it did *after* the events in Goulston Street, perhaps accounts for his suppressing it.

Major Henry Smith had no such qualms, however, concerning the evidence of one Joseph Lawende, a commercial traveller of German origin, who upon leaving the Imperial Club in Duke Street at 1.35 a.m. saw in Church Passage, one of the three ways into and out of Mitre Square, a man and woman talking together. According to Cullen, the description issued by the City Police, was of a man . . . *about thirty years of age, five feet nine inches tall, with a fair moustache, who was dressed in something like navy serge, and a deerstalker hat; also a red neckerchief.* The major is reported as being satisfied that Lawende returned a true bill of the Ripper, pointing out in substantiation that . . . it was bright moonlight, almost as light as day.

By the time Donald Rumbelow came to research the incident, via the *Police Gazette*, the clothing had faded somewhat into . . . *a pepper and salt colour*, while the deer-stalker has diminished to a . . . *grey cloth cap with a peak of the same material.* The man himself is described as . . . *looking like a sailor.*

Left: A flower-seller, still young and attractive, offering her kerb-side wares. In the autumn of 1888 the Cries of London *were all too frequently "Murder ! 'Orrible Murder ! By courtesy City of London Guildhall Library.*

Robin Odell goes further, adding that the man's moustache was . . . *waxed and pointed*, and that . . . *he did not have the bearing of a Briton, or of a Frenchman, or a German, but was definitely foreign!* A little more licence and the subject could have acquired a robe with a cowl and been transformed into Brother Martin, the mad monk who in 1530 allegedly seized a woman by the throat and, on the very spot where Eddowes was done away with, hacked her to pieces with a knife before treading her out of all recognition.

If, however, we stick to Cullen's description and set it alongside that attributed by Rumbelow to Steve White, a young policeman on special duty near Mitre Square on the night Eddowes was killed, the differences are not very marked . . . *about five feet ten inches in height . . . evidently a man who had seen better days . . . his face was long and thin, nostrils rather delicate, and his hair was jet black. His complexion was inclined to be sallow, and altogether the man was foreign in appearance . . . about thirty-three, at the most.* Which, in turn, is not dissimilar to the description offered later on by a witness called Hutchinson concerning an incident in Dorset Street, or for that matter that given by Mrs. Long, following Annie Chapman's death.

Actually each description owes something to the other, and if one picks out the common factors the result may well be a fairly accurate Identikit of Jack the Ripper.

Another conflict of evidence that bedevilled matters was the time of finding and the characteristics of a knife picked up in Whitechapel Road some time after the Mitre Square outrage; one writer has it that it was . . . *later the same morning*, and was . . . *razor sharp*; another that it was . . . *not until the early hours of Monday*, and that it was . . . *too blunt to be the murder weapon*. Perhaps, had speculation been continued, it could have been traced to Brother Martin!

It must have been in just such a mood of mixed frustration and despair that the police finally withdrew their cordon, for as the autumn dawn washed over the sands of recent events, so must the Ripper's shadowy outline have seemed to grow more blurred, until, in the full light of day, so faded became his image that, were it not for his leavings, he might not have existed.

Episode Six: Shadows Between

I'm not a butcher,
I'm not a Yid,
Nor yet a foreign skipper,
But I'm your own light-hearted friend,
Yours truly, Jack the Ripper.

Now of all the communications sent to the police and others that were signed thus, or otherwise purported to come from the Whitechapel murderer, the overwhelming majority constituted the outpourings of cranks or pranksters; some, however, were less obviously the product of sick or irresponsible minds, and of these just three have come to be taken seriously by most investigators. The first such – and this, incidentally, was the first time the name Jack the Ripper had been employed – was received at the *Central News Agency* on the 28th of September, but was not published until after the Stride-Eddowes murders two days later. The letter, the envelope of which bore a London East Central postmark, was dated the 25th of September and read:

> Dear Boss
>
> I keep on hearing the police have caught me but they wont fix me just yet. I have laughed when they look so clever and talk about being on the right track. That joke about Leather Apron [Leather Apron was a suspect] gave me real fits. I am down on whores and I shan't quit ripping them till I do get buckled. Grand work the last job was. I gave the lady no time to squeal. How can they catch me now. I love my work and want to start again. You will soon hear of me with my funny little games. I saved some of the proper red stuff in a ginger beer bottle over the last job to write with but it went thick like glue and I can't use it. Red ink is fit enough I hope ha ha.
> The next job I do I shall clip the ladys ears off and send to the police officers just for jolly wouldnt you. Keep this letter back till I do a bit more work, then give it out straight. My knife's so nice and sharp I want to get to work right away if I get a chance. Good luck.
>
> Yours truly
> Jack the Ripper
>
> Dont mind me giving the trade name

And at right angles to the letter proper:

> wasnt good enough to post this before I got all the red ink off my hands curse it
> No luck yet. They say I'm a doctor now ha ha

31

A second communication, this time written on a postcard and also signed Jack the Ripper, reached the *Central News Agency* after the murders in Berner Street and Mitre Square, and ran as follows:

> *I was not codding dear old boss when I gave you the tip, you ll hear about saucy Jacky s work tomorrow double ev-ent this time number one squealed a bit couldnt finish straight off. had no time to get the ears for police thanks for keeping last letter back till I got to work again,*
>
> Jack the Ripper

The letter and postcard were penned in quite different and distinct hands, the one neatly rounded and looped, with a uniform forward slant, the other bolder, almost letter-spaced, and nearly upright. Yet – and this notwithstanding that the letter had not been published before the postcard was already committed to the post – the second communication alluded positively to the contents of the first . . . *had no time to get the ears for police*, and . . . *thanks for keeping last letter back.*

The postcard also spoke specifically of a . . . *double ev-ent this time*, which, taken together with the comment . . . *number one squealed a bit couldnt finish straight off*, has been proof enough for most writers – reacting to the assumption that the postcard was mailed on Sunday, September 30th, the day before details of the Stride murder were generally known – that the author and the killer were one and the same. It followed that the killer was also responsible for the first letter and that Jack the Ripper had coined his own *nom de guerre*.

Until recently that is, when Stephen Knight added his voice to that of the too often disregarded Leonard Matters in declaring that the postcard was, in fact, franked as October the 1st, which meant that it could have been – and probably was – posted a day, or part of a day, later than has hitherto been supposed; late enough, at any rate, for its author to know the pertinent details of the so-called double event.

Thus, it may be argued, if the postcard is suspect so, *ipso facto*, is the letter that preceded it. However, while on the evidence so far presented it is perfectly proper to play piggy-back with these two inter-related missives, it is not so to indulge in a game of leap-frog and conclude that because the postcard is suspect, it and the letter are false. Suffice it to say that if they are genuine there is to be reconciled the very real difficulty presented by the two sets of handwriting, while if they are false there is room to wonder at the timely and predictive nature of the letter and to speculate afresh as to its source.

THE NEMESIS OF NEGLECT. Here the real villain of the piece is depicted as the ever-present spectre of neglect and squalor. Printed by Punch, or the London Charivari, Sept. 29th, 1888, and reproduced by courtesy of Punch Publications Limited.

There is no doubt about the writer's spelling ability, and it is apparent that, despite his general parsimony over punctuation marks, he can employ the apostrophe well enough when it escapes his attention not to do so. The overall impression is, if not of an educated hand in the public school or university sense, of someone who has reached a high level of literacy and is, moreover, a fluent wordsmith with a working knowledge of fringe-element slang – someone like a newspaper reporter, for example.

The newsworld connotations are perhaps heightened by the fact that both the letter and the postcard were sent to the *Central News Agency*, and one is bound to ask whether a couple of enterprising journalists did not concoct the undertaking in an attempt to keep the public pot boiling after the Chapman Murder, and simply struck lucky with their timing, or whether there is not another, less cut and dried, possibility?

In tieing the letter to the postcard, and vice-versa, and irrespective of their being genuine or not, the knotting of the twine has always depended on the assumption that the contents of the letter were not published until after the postcard was beyond recall. But published is not the same thing as divulged. What an intriguing situation it would present if betwixt the *Central News Agency* and the eventual recipients of its newsgathering, a third party came into possession of the letter and made improper use of it? Were this so, only the second communication – that embodied in the postcard – becomes demonstrably spurious. One thing is certain, any legitimate doubt cast on its authenticity must endorse the question mark placed earlier in this narrative against the name of Elizabeth Stride as a *bona-fide*, beyond-any-shadow-of-a-doubt Ripper victim.

The third communication on our shortening short-list was sent to Mr. George Lusk, chairman of the *Whitechapel Vigilance Committee*, which had come into being after the murder of Annie Chapman. This letter, which was a mass of sweeping downstrokes shudderingly like those of a confidently weilded knife, had about it an air of arrogant spontaneity, as if its writer didn't give a damn. But, then, bearing in mind the place from whence the letter came, this last is hardly surprising:

> *From hell*
>
> *Mr Lusk*
> *Sir*
> *I send you half the Kidne I took from one women prasarved it for you tother piece I fried and ate it was very nise. I may send you the bloody knif that took it out if you only wate a whil longer*
>
> *signed*
>
> *Catch me when you can*
> *Mishter Lusk*

Now this letter was received on October the 16th, and it did contain part of a kidney, which was subsequently examined and pronounced upon by Dr. Oppenshaw, the Pathological Curator of the *London Hospital Museum*. His findings were that . . . *it was a "ginny" kidney from a woman of about forty-five*, and that . . . *it had been removed within the last three weeks. It exhibited clinical signs of an advanced state of Bright's disease* [a degenerative condition marked by a diminution of the organ's active blood vessels], *and had appended to it one inch of the renal artery.* It only remained to compare the specimen with what was known about Catherine Eddowes to arrive at a conclusion.

Where the one was "ginny", the other was known to be a chronic alcoholic; where the one had belonged to a middle-aged female, the other was forty-three; where the one was less than three weeks removed, the other had been dead just under that length of time; where the one exhibited changes consistent with Bright's disease, the other suffered from that complaint; and finally, where the one retained just one inch of renal artery, the other had been left with two of the three inches that normally constitutes the whole of that vessel.

Not this time, therefore, are we concerned with postal dates and the possession, or otherwise, of esoteric knowledge, but with the matching halves of the Ripper's indentures – proof positive, surely, of an apprenticeship successfully served and gruesomely authenticated.

Reproduction of the letter sent to Mr. Lusk, a type-set copy of which appears on facing page.

Episode Seven: Dead End

It is approaching 10.45 a.m. on Friday, the ninth day of November, when Thomas Bowyer, having failed to budge the door of No. 13 Miller's Court, off Dorset Street, turns instead to an adjacent window. Thwarted again, this time on account of some material hung from the inside, Bowyer reaches through a broken pane and relieves the covering. What he sees in the room beyond is enough to stun even his slum-blunted sensibilities.

On the solitary bed, the trappings belonging to which are heaped with some blood-stained garments at its foot, lies the naked form of what was once a young and, by East End standards, pre-possessing woman. That Black Mary Kelly – so called because of her long raven hair – will never now pay the overdue rent that Thomas Bowyer has been sent to collect, is patent, for not only has her throat been cut as far back as the spinal column and her ears and nose amputated, but the face is so ravaged as almost to defy recognition.

The body is an equally revolting spectacle, with the stomach and abdomen rent asunder and some of the contents removed to a bed-side table. Here, displayed like offerings at a cannibal's feast, are . . . Black Mary's breasts, her heart and her kidneys, while in closer proximity to the body, as if the most recently lifted from its human chafing-dish, is the dead woman's liver.

Although the police and other officials are quickly at the scene, it is not until 1.30 p.m. that they eventually force the door and enter Kelly's room. Once inside, it is apparent that the carnage wrought there transcends in bestiality anything that even the most hardened among them has ever witnessed. Even the walls are flecked with blood, a gruesome underdrop to the obscene frieze of flesh that depends in raw lumps from the protruding picture-frame nails.

What is not apparent at this time is that in their subsequent investigations the police are to be confronted with evidence that places one vital piece of the bloody jig-saw, that of Black Mary herself, in two places at the same time, thereby creating a conundrum couched in a contradiction that endures to this day.

36

Friday, the ninth day of November in the year eighteen-hundred and eighty-eight, was not, in any case, intended to be an ordinary day; it was the day when the Lord Mayor-elect, the Rt. Honourable James Whitehead, would ride through the City of London in his gilded coach; it was, moreover, a day when the First Citizen to-be would display his magnanimity by tossing to the watching poor copper and silver coin of the realm, as transitory a lining of their empty pockets as, later, would be the filling of their bellies with a meat pie supper at the *Great Assembly Hall* in Mile End Road.

Was it, then, by chance that Jack the Ripper chose this same day to strike down his latest victim, and in such a manner as to steal both the Lord Mayor's Show and the newspaper headlines? Or did he do so because he could do no other, because he had reached that penultimate stage along the road to total madness that will brook no opposition? One thing is certain, in acting as he did the Ripper proved himself a shrewder judge of East Enders than did James Whitehead, for while all the latter could bestow upon them was his patronage and a pauper's pie, Jack could offer them something they could feed off for the rest of their lives – his contempt.

Thus, while City dignitaries dusted off their plumage in readiness for the morrow, Jack the Ripper was waiting in the wings, stalking his intended victim as early, perhaps, as the evening before when the twenty-four year old Mary Jane Kelly, her bold blue eyes glazed with drink and her black hair hanging loose to a waist that was beginning to thicken with a three month pregnancy, was seen in, and then leaving, the *Britannia* public house in Dorset Street. The man she was with was almost a cartoon figure, being . . . *short and stout, with a blotchy face and a full carroty moustache. He was about thirty-eight years of age, and wore a round billycock hat.* Apart from his distinctive appearance, it was noticed that he was carrying some beer in a bucket – the Victorian equivalent of a "pail" ale, no doubt !

The Widow Cox, who, like Kelly, lived in one of the six hovels flanking Miller's Court which were known as *McCarthy's Rents,* saw the pair enter the girl's quarters at approximately 11.45 p.m., after which time she heard Kelly's maudlin voice lifted in song. According to the widow, Kelly was still singing fifteen minutes later when she, the Widow Cox, went out, as indeed was the case when she returned at about 1.00 a.m. By now it was raining, but a few minutes later she quit the premises yet again, cheered no doubt by the strains of whatever tune Mary Kelly was now rendering and the light in her window. When Cox finally returned to *McCarthy's Rents* at about 3.00 a.m., No. 13 Miller's Court was as dark and as silent as the grave.

Left: Dorset Street (Stanford's Map of London), and Overleaf: The Lord Mayor's Procession, 9 November, 1888, from an oil painting by W. Logsdail. Both reproduced by courtesy City of London Guildhall Library.

Fortunately for the man in the billycock hat, Kelly was seen abroad by another witness mid-way between the hours of one and three. George Hutchinson, an out-of-work night watchman, was on the streets at 2.00 a.m., when, on the corner of Thrawl Street, he spotted Kelly, whom he knew well, take up with a man. Hutchinson was to make a statement to the police that the man was . . . *about thirty-five years of age and some five feet six inches in height, with a pale complexion and dark eyes and eye lashes. His hair was dark also, and he had a slight moustache curled up at either end.* He *was surly looking and wore a long dark coat, trimmed at collar and cuffs with astrakhan, over a dark jacket, light waistcoat and dark trousers. His dark felt hat was turned down in the middle, and he had button boots and gaiters fastened by white buttons.* The rest of his ensemble consisted of . . . *a linen collar and a black tie fastened with a horse-shoe pin. He also affected a thick gold chain across his front, and walked very briskly.* Other accounts add to the gold chain a seal with a red stone.

For reasons best known to himself, George Hutchinson followed the couple to Dorset Street, where the man indulged in some byplay with a red handkerchief before they turned up the court towards No. 13. It must now have been about 2.15 a.m., and after hanging about for another forty-five minutes, Hutchinson slouched off. His going, if his story was accurate, must, therefore, have been at about the same time as the Widow Cox was on her way back to Miller's Court at 3.00 a.m. There is, however, no record of them meeting.

And that, to all intents and purposes, should have been that; and would have been had not another witness alleged seeing Mary Kelly alive at a time when she was presumed to be dead. Caroline Maxwell was the wife of a lodging-house keeper at No. 14 Dorset Street, directly across from Miller's Court, and she was to testify at the inquest on Kelly that she had seen and spoken with the dead woman at eight o'clock on Friday morning. Mrs. Maxwell went further, claiming to have seen Kelly again some three-quartets of an hour later outside the *Britannia* talking to . . . *a stout man dressed in a plaid coat.* Kelly, she said, was wearing . . . *a dark shirt, a velvet body, a maroon shawl and no hat.* An attempt by the police to discredit the witness, by stressing that the identification was made at a distance of twenty-five yards, is put in its proper perspective if one appreciates that today that is the distance at which the Road Traffic Act requires a driver to be able to read the registration number of another vehicle.

Mrs. Maxwell's evidence was more seriously challenged by certain circumstantial evidence, also given at the inquest, first by Elizabeth Prater, a prostitute who repaired to her room directly above Mary Kelly's at a little before 1.30 a.m. At that time she heard and saw nothing untoward, not even a light in Kelly's window; but between 3.30 a.m. and 3.45 a.m., when she was disturbed in her sleep, she heard a faint cry of "Oh, murder", coming, as she thought, from the court below. Philosophically, Prater turned over and went back to sleep, not wakening again until 5.00 a.m., when she rose and was in the *Ten Bells* by a quarter to six.

Sarah Lewis, a laundress, also recounted her recollection of events in and around Miller's Court in the nether hours. At 2.30 a.m., as she turned into the court to visit a Mrs. Keyler who lived opposite Kelly, she observed loitering there . . . *a stout man of middle height wearing a black wide-awake hat.* This may or may no have been Hutchinson, but what Mrs. Lewis was sure about was that after she awoke from a doze in one of Mrs. Keyler's fireside chairs, she heard the clock of Christ Church, Spitalfields, striking half-past three. She remained awake, and at nearly four o'clock heard a loud cry of "Murder". It sounded, she said, just outside; there was only the one scream, and it was the voice of a young woman. Like Elizabeth Prater, Sarah Lewis took no more notice.

As was to be expected, the gregarious Widow Cox added her mite to the Miller's Court chorus, her contribution being that after hearing a man who worked in the Spitalfields market leave for work, she heard another man go down the court at 6.15 a.m. Led by the Coroner, she agreed that . . . *as she heard no door bang behind him, he must have walked up the court and then back again – a policeman, perhaps.* Such was the quality of question and answer that sought to throw light on the murder of Dark Mary Kelly.

So, far from being an unfrequented back alley during the hours of darkness, Miller's Court was a veritable hive of activity, with folk coming and going at all hours; in fact, there was probably more traffic in and out of the court during the early part of the morning than there was later on, a circumstance that will bear closer scrutiny in due course.

In the meantime, it is relevant to enquire as to how the police came to be so tardy in commencing their investigation, and what conclusions were reached when they did commence it. The delay in effecting an entry to Kelly's room was occasioned by a decree issued by Sir Charles Warren of such monumental stupidity that, by comparison, Nelson's column might be regarded as Lilliputian. In it, the Commissioner insisted that . . . *in the event of another Ripper murder the police were to do nothing until the arrival of* Barnaby *and* Burgho, *two bloodhounds with whose reputed sagacity he had lately become much impressed.* What his ham-strung officers did not know was that Sir Charles had just tendered his resignation to the then Home Secretary, and that the hounds were, in any case, unavailable.

Such delay was, of course, inimical to the police investigation from the start; not only did it obscure the time of the victim's death in an elastic shroud of doubt that may be pulled first this way and then that, but it led to endless, and unprofitable, speculation concerning the significance of a fire in Kelly's grate, the remains of which at 1.30 p.m. were still warm. This led to the supposition that the Ripper had built and sustained a fierce fire in the light of which he could act out his nightmare. A fire so fierce that it melted and deformed the extremities of a heat-girt kettle? A fire so flambuoyant that the light of its leaping flames did not penetrate the imperfect covering at the window and impinge upon the path of those who passed through Miller's Court at material times? A fire so prolonged that, although it appeared to have fed on nothing more tangible than what had belonged to the wire frame of a felt hat, and some other odds and ends of clothing, its embers were still warm many hours later? A fire that was, apparently, necessary to see by, when a candle in the same room remained unlit?

How different a complexion would be placed on matters if, in response to these questions, it could be said that . . . there was no proof that the dilapidated kettle was not in that condition prior to the night and morning of November the eight and ninth, that . . . the light from the flames was not seen during the hours of darkness because, like the dog in the Sherlock Holmes story that did not bark, the light did not shine, that . . . the embers were still warm on Friday afternoon simply because Kelly herself had had a fire in her room, but at a later time and of a more modest nature than was generally supposed.

This, however, would be to believe Mrs. Maxwell at the expense of the medical evidence. Or would it? Leonard Matters, in the first serious book on the Ripper, perhaps beguiled future writers into making false assumptions when he declares . . . *Dr. George Bagster Phillips did not enter the room at that moment, and there was no need for him to do so. The bed . . . was quite close to the window and . . . it was apparent to him that Kelly had been dead some five or six hours at least.* Thus, at some time after 11.00 a.m., did the police surgeon for the Whitechapel Division practise his forensic skills as through a glass darkly.

Cullen is hardly more helpful, contenting himself with recording that . . . *Mrs. Maxwell's evidence was so at variance with the known facts that the Coroner cautioned her to be very careful.* Cullen, in turn, admonishes the Coroner by pointing out that . . . *he concluded without thinking fit to ask the surgeon if parts of the body were missing or about the nature of the wounding.* He might have added, as Stephen Knight later did, *or the time of death.*

Donald Rumbelow is less coy, stating unequivocally that . . . *a large fire had been burning in the grate. The ashes were still warm, even seven hours after the estimated time that the Ripper had probably left the house.* He also declares . . . *from the medical and other evidence, the time of death had been established at being between 3.30 a.m. and 4.00 a.m.,* but elsewhere quotes fully from a special report prepared by Dr. Thomas Bond, who besides being a lecturer on Forensic Medicine was also

ANOTHER MISS! A typical lampoon by Fun Magazine *(October 3, 1888) showing Home Secretary Matthews and General Sir Charles Warren bemused at their joint failure to bag the Ripper.*

consulting surgeon to A-Division and one of the large railway companies, to the effect that . . . *death took place . . . about one or two o'clock in the morning.*

Stephen Knight, who is otherwise rarely vague, writes . . . *Mrs. Maxwell's assertion that she saw Kelly at 9.00 a.m., when medical evidence shows she had been dead for five or six hours when her body was found at 10.45 a.m., is one of the enduring mysteries concerning the Ripper case.*

Daniel Farson dismisses the problem in a couple of sentences . . . *you will notice that Mary Kelly was seen to be alive after she was dead. This merely confirms what the police always say, that eye-witnesses are notoriously unreliable.* So, it seems, are medical reports, especially those which are heard beyond closed doors.

There is some difficulty also over a door of another kind, for notwithstanding that the key to the one in Kelly's room appears to have been lost for some little time, the door was said to be both locked and bolted when the police broke in. There are two obvious possibilities: that the killer doubly secured the door from within and escaped through the window, and that he locked and bolted the door from outside, reaching, as Kelly and her intimates were known to do, through the broken window to accomplish the latter. As Rumbelow insists . . . *someone had a key.* And even if this were not so and the door was only bolted, this, too, would point to someone other than a stranger unless the window was, in fact, used as a means of egress.

A mystery of another kind surrounded the inquest on Mary Jane Kelly held in Shoreditch Town Hall on Monday, the twelfth day of November, before Coroner Robert MacDonald. It commenced with an unseemly procedural wrangle as to its location in Shoreditch when death had occurred within the bailiwick of the able, if waspish, Mr. Wynn E. Baxter, and ended with MacDonald refusing to hear detailed evidence in open court, and, indeed, adjourning the hearing on the day it began.

There are those who allege that both MacDonald and Bagster Phillips were puppets in a cover-up, and there is no doubt that the Coroner did act unconstitutionally, a fact which most writers on the subject admit but do not pursue. Stephen Knight alone goes so much further, and beneath his pen the Shoreditch cover-up assumes truly Watergate proportions. Why else, he asks, would the inquest have been wrested from its lawful venue, unless it was that in Baxter the authorities would have had to contend with a man who would not be gagged, a man who would have insisted in sifting every last detail before the public eye and ear, and who would, if the course of his duty so dictated, not have hesitated to expose those who were in breach of the law? Why else should the more pliant MacDonald, aided and abetted by George Bagster Phillips, have so maladroitly swept the inquest aside in no more time than is occupied by a pantomime matinee? Why else should the police, thereafter, have ceased to pursue their enquiries, if not because they knew, or were informed, that the Ripper's day was done?

Each of these questions can be equally well answered by extrapolating the consequences of Sir Charles Warren's obsession with a potential public disturbance on a massive scale. The facts are, he *was* fearful of an insurrection; he did stand aghast at the prospect of an ethnic bloodbath between Jew and Gentile, and in the light of his state of mind it is understandable, if not excusable, that he should act as he did and cause others to act likewise. As to the police, there is no doubt that morale was at its lowest ebb; they were lampooned in the press, abused in the streets, and denigrated at every turn.

Now, the very man who had brought them to this pass had deserted them, departing from office, it was said, in a fit of pique following a rift between himself and an equally inept Home Secretary, but in truth driven out by the evil genius of Jack the Ripper. And even if nature does abhor a vacuum, the one bequeathed the police by Sir Charles was not easily or quickly filled; the poison had gone too deep, and their apathy was symptomatic of its virulence.

Ironically, the Ripper may also have created a vacuum, one so perfect that in the destruction of Kelly and her foetus he reached his climactic, never to kill again. Except perhaps himself. If this was so, who is to say that the paths of the police and Jack the Ripper did not journey into limbo that November Friday, or that each in their separate way did not reach the same . . . dead end?

Episode Eight: Shadows After

With the killing of Mary Jane Kelly the day of the Ripper was indeed done, and although the East End of London was yet to suffer many brutal murders, some of them of the most terrible kind, none were to be as comprehensively horrific, as emphatically evil, as those undertaken by Jack the Ripper between the last day of August and the ninth day of November. Neither was any future murder to find the police so poorly led, in such low spirits, and so alienated from the public.

In the last quarter of the nineteenth century Scotland Yard detectives were still living down the stigma bequeathed by the corrupt and incompetent Bow Street Runners, and were denied even the grudging, if hostile, respect accorded to uniformed officers by the working classes. Writers of the period varied in their attitude to the police, but were generally antipathetic; even Conan Doyle portrayed Holmes' opposite numbers as sly rather than intelligent. The truth is that the operational ranks of both the uniform and detective branches in Victorian times were filled, for the most part, by able and concientious officers; it is a matter for regret that they did not enjoy leadership of an equal calibre at executive level.

The Ripper case, from the police point of view, could not have got off to a more inauspicious start, for on the day following the murder of Annie Chapman in Hanbury Street Sir Robert Anderson, the newly appointed Assistant Commissioner of the Metropolitan Police and head of the Criminal Investigation Department, was on his way to a winter holiday in Switzerland. His chief and sponsor, the then Commissioner of the Metropolitan Police, Sir Charles Warren, had been instrumental in removing Anderson's predecessor, the independent-minded and experienced James Monro, just over a week previously, and the overall result now was that there were two unsolved murders in the Whitechapel area of London, with no-one to take charge of the situation. No-one other than Sir Charles Warren himself, that is.

Warren, an ex-Major-General of Engineers, had brought to the Metropolitan Police Force a brand of militarism that did nothing for the morale of his men, and less for the confidence of the populace. In the days of British Imperialism, it was perhaps inevitable that an ex-general should use, or threaten to use, force on occasion, but to promise it on the least provocation was to strain to breaking point the already brittle relationship between police and public – particularly the East End public – and to ensure that when the test came there would be lacking that degree of trust and cooperation that might have brought the Ripper to heel.

As it was, the police arrested more than a hundred and sixty suspects – and had to release them; descended upon untold numbers of common lodging-houses and sleazy slums – and came away empty handed (if not without addition to their persons!); followed up every lead and likelihood – and reached a dead end. Five dead ends, in fact, for none of the slayings yielded an indictable suspect.

Between the Nichols and Chapman murders, the police learned that a man called Jack Pizer, known as Leather Apron, had been knocking prostitutes about, and it was natural that suspicion should be intensified when, at the scene of the Chapman murder, was found the article of the nick-name. Then, when Timothy Donovan, Annie Chapman's lodging-house keeper, recalled seeing Pizer in a deer-stalker hat similar to that worn by the man seen in Hanbury Street on the morning of the murder, Pizer was traced to No. 22 Mulberry Street and arrested there on Monday, the tenth day of September. Several suggestively sharp, long-bladed knives were found, but these were, Pizer protested, tools of his boot-finishing trade and had no bearing on the deaths of Nichols or Chapman. The upshot was that Pizer was taken to and eventually released from Leman Street police station, being so vindicated in the process that he thereafter commenced, and in due course successfully concluded, actions for libel against several over-eager newspapers.

At the same time as Jack Pizer was being detained at Leman Street, William Piggott, a man who featured Pizer to some extent, was at Commercial Street police station, also being interrogated – one might almost say gated-in-terror, so large and hostile was the mob without. Piggott, however, was found to be innocent but insane and was bundled off to an asylum.

Another unfortunate at the wrong end of the public's pointing finger was a mad pork butcher called Joseph Isenschmid. This man, who had the unnerving habit of carrying about with him several fearsome-looking knives, was harried and hounded unmercifully, finally establishing his innocence by virtue of the fact that he was in the Bow Infirmary asylum when the Ripper struck again. Mrs. Isenschmid had earlier spoken stoutly in defence of her husband when she remarked, "I do not think he would injure anyone but me."

Throughout the serial murders the minor suspects came and went. There was William Nichols, Polly Nichols' estranged husband; there was John Richardson – he who had looked into the yard behind No. 29 Hanbury Street and thus confounded the findings of the police surgeon as to the time of Annie Chapman's death; there was the unfortunately named Michael Kidney, with whom Elizabeth Stride cohabited; there was John Kelly, who had been living with Catherine Eddowes for the past seven years, and who had just returned with her from a hop-picking expedition in Kent, an excursion which they had terminated early because Eddowes thought she knew the identity of the Ripper and might get the reward money. Her knowledge seems to have evaporated as quickly as her earnings from the hop fields, for when the couple parted on the night before Eddowes was murdered she had made neither an accusation nor provision for her bed. And finally there was Joseph Barnett, with whom Black Mary Kelly normally shared her room at No. 13 Miller's Court. It was Barnett who, during the course of a violent quarrel with Kelly, had broken the window through which, later on, so many came to peer at her corpse.

But prospects of this calibre had no permanent place in the Ripper rogues' gallery, and as one century turned into the next, so the shape and substance of the Ripper murders faded into the chameleon of time, and it was not until comparatively recent years that a rash of writers embarked upon the task of presenting a parade of more sophisticated suspects. What follows, therefore, is what might properly be termed . . . A Review of Retrospective Rippers:

No. 1. DRUITT, Montague John: M. J. Druitt was born at Wimborne, Dorset, on August 15th, 1857, which makes him just thirty-one years of age when the Whitechapel murders commenced. The son of well-to-do parents (his father William was the leading surgeon in the locality), he was educated at Winchester, where he excelled at cricket, and at New College, Oxford, from which he emerged with a moderate B.A. degree in 1880.

Turning to the law, Druitt was admitted to the Inner Temple in May, 1882, and was called to the Bar, before the Inns of Court benchers, in 1885, taking chambers at No. 9 King's Bench Walk, which he retained throughout the rest of his lifetime. Unfortunately, success in his chosen career eluded him, and the part-time post he had taken sometime previously, at a crammer in Blackheath, soon became his permanent means of livelihood; until the end of the Michaelmas term in 1888, that is, when, for reasons unknown, he was dismissed.

This period of Druitt's life – between the autumns of 1885 and 1888 – was harrowing in the extreme, for not only did his father die but his mother was confined to an asylum at Chiswick. Montague John himself was seen last alive on Monday, the 3rd of December, 1888, and his fully-clothed body was recovered from the Thames at Thornycroft's, near Chiswick, precisely four weeks later, on Monday, the 31st of December. Meanwhile, at Druitt's chambers was discovered a letter addressed to his brother William, saying, "Since Friday I felt I was going to be like mother and the best thing for me was to die".

The Evictions in Leather Lane, December 1891. Such scenes were commonplace in the East End, with entire families turned into the street to make shift as best they could. By courtesy City of London Guildhall Library.

The case against Montague John Druitt has been built, in the main, by Tom Cullen and Daniel Farson, and the latter, in particular, relies upon notes copied from notes originated by Sir Melville MacNaghten, in which he allegedly wrote . . . *I enumerate the cases of three men against whom the police held very reasonable suspicion. Personally . . . I am inclined to exonerate two of them.*

Stephen Knight, however, in his exhaustive inquiry into this aspect of the case, is able to quote verbatim from MacNaghten's *original* writings . . . *many homicidal maniacs were suspected, but no shadow of proof could be thrown at any one. I may mention the cases of three men, any one of whom would have been more likely than Cutbush* [another latter-day suspect] *to have committed this series of murders.*

So there we have it, a clear declaration, not of certitude but of official ignorance, six years after the fact by a man who came to office when the Ripper's reign was over. Far from implicating Druitt, who was, in fact, one of the three men MacNaghten referred to earlier in his notes, this same official was, in effect, indicating the absolute absence of evidence against Druitt to illuminate the absurdity of the allegations made in respect of Cutbush.

In furtherance of his argument, Farson holds that in another copy of MacNaghten's notes – those made by his daughter – there are the words . . . *I have always held strong opinions regarding No. 1 (Druitt) and the more I think the matter over, the stronger do these opinions become. The truth, however, will never be known, and did indeed at one time lie at the bottom of the Thames . . .*

This page does not, according to Knight, appear in the original notes, and there are, he claims, other discrepancies. In the genuine article, for instance, there is no mention of Druitt's age at the time of his death, simply that he was found in the river . . . *on December 31st,* whereas Farson states, in his first book, that it was December 3rd, and in his revised version that it was December 13th.

Words of another complexion are introduced when, in seeking to consolidate the case against Druitt, Farson succeeds in mortally wounding his own. Having traced Montague John's cousin Dr. Lionel Druitt to Australia in 1887, Farson refers to a letter he received from that country, from a Mr. Knowles, concerning a document he had once seen, titled *The East End Murderer – I Knew Him,* by a Lionel Drewett, Drewery or Druitt, published by a Mr. Fell of Dandenong, in 1890.

Unfortunately, Farson lost the letter and there is no record of Mr. Knowles's address, and, therefore, no means of putting to him certain relevant and searching questions. To leap, as Farson and the Druittites do, from a third-time-lucky choice of name to a positive family link between the author and

Montague John, and thence to Montague John himself as being the Ripper, is rather like landing on the moon without benefit of rocket propulsion.

Next we are asked to hark back to cousin Lionel's whereabouts before he emigrated to Australia. According to Farson, Dr. Lionel Druitt... *had a surgery at the Minories in 1879 . . . and it is reasonable to assume that Montague might have visited him there . . . It is conceivable that he even lived there himself after Lionel had gone, and that at some time Lionel had grounds for suspicion.*

In fact, Dr. Druitt was not domiciled in the Minories in 1879, being there for a few months only in the capacity of assistant to another doctor. Actually, between 1879 and 1889 the address in the Minories was occupied by doctors who had no known connection with either Lionel Druitt or with Montague John Druitt. To speculate that the latter might have resided there is to credit him with more ample means than his circumstances allow, particularly as from 1885 onwards he had chambers at No. 9 King's Bench Walk to maintain.

Montague of the Minories is, in fact, one of the outstanding red-herrings to be drawn across the trail of Jack the Ripper, and owes its provenance, in part, to a letter written from Liverpool on September 29th, 1888:

> *Beware, I shall be at work on the 1st and 2nd inst., in Minories at twelve midnight, and I give the authorities a good chance, but there is never a policeman near when I am at Work.*

And also from Liverpool, after the double event of September 30th:

> *What fools the police are. I even give them the name of the street where I am living.*

Yet it is remarkable what such an obviously maloderous, twice-cast piece of bait can achieve, for, although previous researchers had wrinkled their noses and turned away from it, the Druittites equate it with the work of the Ripper and the Ripper with Montague John, linking "the street where I am living" with the Minories and not with that at the top of the first letter, which was Prince William Street, Liverpool.

Finally, we come to Druitt's state of mind. Clearly it was disturbed, as witness the suicide note left for his brother William. But why should it not have been? His father had died, his mother, whom he seems to have visited at Chiswick just prior to his death, was in an asylum, and his own fortunes were at a low ebb. This, however, does not conjure up, in one sweep of the psychoanalytical wand, the picture of a man either so manic or so paranoid that he was wont to sally forth at intervals and butcher a passing prostitute.

Nor is it possible, with equal facility, to subscribe to the theory that because Druitt's own family perhaps suspected him of being the Whitechapel murderer his own kin did away with him, and that his brother William, then the epitome of respectability as a seaside solicitor, master-minded the deed.

No. 2. Stanley, Doctor: In his book *The Mystery of Jack the Ripper,* Leonard Matters posed three vital questions: Why were the Ripper victims all prostitutes? Why did the Ripper hunt only in the East End of London? Why did the Ripper cease killing after the death of Black Mary Kelly? His answers were models of simplicity: Because it was among *them* that he would find the woman he sought; because it was *there* that she would be· because Mary Kelly was *the* woman in question.

According to Matters, Dr. Stanley was a brilliant surgeon who became a distinguished one, a career that was blighted when his wife died and left him with an infant son. His interests, always intense, became morbid, and he developed an obsession with the pathological aspects of cancer, believing that his son would, ultimately, master the scourge and deliver suffering humanity from its toils.

Eventually, young Herbert Stanley, when a medical student of twenty-one – and as brilliant as his father had predicted – met and dallied with a girl only a year older than himself, learning too late that she was diseased. Herbert was infected and the virus soon took a firm hold, for, although his father discovered what had happened only a few weeks after the fact, the remedial action taken by him, and by the finest specialists in the land, proved of no avail, and two years later Herbert Stanley was dead.

So far so bad. In the first place, it is extraordinary for venereal disease to develop such a rapidly fatal course; and in the second place, there was no indication, at the *post mortem* on Kelly, that she was infected. She might, of course, have been a carrier, in which case the disease could equally effectively have been transmitted to young Stanley, bringing us back to the fundamental weakness in Matters' story – that its onset and conclusion was so uncharacteristically swift.

Be this as it may, the Dr. Stanley of the day, having learned that Mary Jane Kelly – known romantically to Herbert as Marie Jeanette – had been the cause of his son's downfall, determined to seek her out in London's East End, and by dint of skill and cunning – *a change of attire; a slovenly gait; a garbled form of English* – to isolate and destroy her. To do so he has recourse to quizzing various street women and then, to cover his tracks, killing them. The first of these was Martha Turner, or Tabram (not generally acknowledged to be a Ripper victim), then Polly Nichols; to be followed, in turn, by Chapman,

51

Stride and Eddowes. It was Catherine Eddowes who, Matters claims, gave the Ripper Kelly's address, an ironical twist of fate when one remembers that Eddowes herself sometimes went by the same name. To those, however, who would fault Matters on the grounds that Dr. Stanley might well have concluded that Eddowes was the Kelly he was seeking, must be stressed the one fact that is so often overlooked – that *the* Kelly was still only twenty-four years of age, whereas Catherine Eddowes was in her forties, and looked much older.

In due course Dr. Stanley corners Mary Kelly in No. 13 Miller's Court and exacts his revenge, escaping thereafter to Buenos Aires, where he confesses to an old pupil of his that he, the once famous Dr. Stanley, is Jack the Ripper. What most Ripperologists are agreed upon is that Matters wrote his book in two distinct halves, a factual, well-researched beginning followed by a thriller-style ending every bit as ficticious as the earlier best-selling Ripper-based novel *The Lodger*, by Marie Belloc Lowndes.

No. 3. Chapman, George (real name Severin Antonovich Klosowski): was born in Poland on December 14th, 1865, where he trained, but did not graduate, as a surgeon before coming to England sometime in 1888. Initially, Klosowski – *Ludwig* Klosowski, as he was now called – worked in Whitechapel as a barber's assistant, with nothing known against him by the police until towards the end of 1902, when, in the name of Chapman, he was arrested and charged in connection with the death of Maud Marsh by antimony poisoning.

That Chapman, or Klosowski, was a cold-blooded murderer, with the deaths of at least two other women on his conscience, is not in doubt. What must be challenged – and vehemently – is his candidature for the bloody mantle of Jack the Ripper, an accolade that was bestowed upon him by Inspector Abberline, one of the senior investigators at case level into the Ripper murders. According to H. L. Adam when he edited *The Trial of George Chapman*, Abberline's words to Chief Inspector Godley, who arrested Chapman, were, *"You've got Jack the Ripper at last!"*

In fact this was almost certainly not so. For one thing, while murderers have been known to modify their method of murder, by no manipulation of the imagination can the mania for mutilation, as exhibited by the Ripper, be reconciled with the passion for poisoning that was Chapman's *modus operandi*. For another, Chapman was, at the time of the Whitechapel glut, only twenty-three years of age, not in itself a total disqualification, but sufficiently at variance with all the known sightings to introduce more than a passing element of doubt.

Subsequently, Inspector Abberline withdrew his allegation, but as so often obtains in matters affecting a man's character – even a murderer's – it is the original remark that is remembered rather than the retraction.

Waiting for the pub to open on a Sunday afternoon. Section of original by courtesy City of London Guildhall Library.

No. 4. Pedachenko, Doctor Alexander: The Pedachenko theory is a complicated one, something that becomes dauntingly apparent when it presents among its *dramatis personae . . . the mad monk Rasputin*; *the Russian Kerensky government*; *the Moscow Ochrana*; *and that romantic journalist and dilletante espionage agent William Le Queux.*

Donald McCormick, in his book *The Identity of Jack the Ripper,* relies heavily on these sources for his material, and also on the writings of Dr. Thomas Dutton. According to McCormick, an entry in Dutton's diary for 1924 reads . . . *What Le Queux should have found out was that Pedachenko worked as a barber-surgeon for a hairdresser named Delhaye in the Westmoreland Road, in 1888.* Well, McCormick did find it out, just as he found that Dr. Dutton's source for his advice to Le Queux was a Dr. J. F. Williams, whom Pedachenko apparently assisted at *St. Saviour's Infirmary.*

Now Dutton was on friendly terms with Inspector Abberline, and – through McCormick – it is Dutton's word we have for it that the Inspector eventually changed his mind about George Chapman being the Ripper, his conversion coming about when he became convinced that Chapman, or Klosowski as he then was, had in London a double, and that this double was in the habit of personating his likeness.

* According to the Le Queux version of McCormick's story, Pedachenko lived at his sister's house in Walworth Road and used to set out from there to carry out his politically-motivated murders, aided and abetted by his friend Levitski and a young tailoress called Winberg. According to Dr. Williams, Pedachenko's voice was . . . *soft and low,* and one remembers that a policeman on duty near Mitre Square the morning Eddowes was murdered spoke to a hurrying figure whose response was . . . *soft and musical.* Earlier, a man answering the Russian's description was allegedly seen in the club in Dutfield's Yard, a man, moreover, who wore . . . *a heavy gold watch chain, with some sort of stone set in a seal; also a peaked hat, rather like a sailor's.*

What if a little later, abroad in Berner Street, this same man called out, not *Lipski,* as the witness Schwartz supposed, but *Levitski,* and that the man with the clay pipe was in fact an accomplice? This would put a new complexion on things, and must add weight to McCormick's theory that Pedachenko, after killing Mary Kelly at Miller's Court, used the water from a boiling kettle to shave off his facial hair, donned some of Kelly's attire, and departed, passing but *not* speaking with Mrs. Caroline Maxwell.

All at once, everybody's evidence is rendered more nearly accurate, starting with that of Israel Schwartz, and concluding with that of Hutchinson, Maxwell and the several women frequenting Miller's Court. The similarity between *Lipski* and *Levitski,* phonetically, is beguiling, and in the light of recent information cannot be dismissed. According to a previous writer, *Lipski* became a vogue word in London in the late 1880s following the death by hanging of a murderer of that name in 1887, yet in response to an enquiry made by the present author, Dr. R. E. Allen, Senior Editor (General) to the Oxford University Press, writes . . . *our files have revealed no evidence of this word used in English contexts.* Neither could Jacqueline Simpson, who did so much work on abridging Eric Partridge's *A Dictionary of Historical Slang,* throw any definitive light on the subject.

So there it is – not a pulling aside of the curtain perhaps, but the slightest of twitches to one of its many folds, a touch so light that it disturbs the mass of material hardly at all; but a touch none-the-less, and one that leaves McCormick's theory deserving of fresh scrutiny

* Certain of this material came to hand as this book was going to press, and space limitations necessitated its being set in a smaller type face.

No. 5. Cream, Doctor Thomas Neill: Cream the Poisoner owes his inclusion as a Ripper suspect, primarily, to his own twisted flair for exhibitionism, when, in 1892, just as Mr. Billington, the Public Hangman, was about to work the drop at Cream's execution for the murder by strychnine poisoning of four London prostitutes, he is said to have exclaimed "*I am Jack –*". Unfortunately, Mr. Billington punctuated the intended sentence a trifle prematurely.

What is not generally known is that during Cream's attendance at the inquest on Matilda Clover, one of his victims, held in the Vestry Hall, Tooting, the coroner, Mr. Braxton Hicks, received a letter which he duly read out. What it amounted to was a tarry-diddle of words proclaiming Cream's innocence and placing the blame on the writer's own shoulders. This communication was, in fact, couched in the same vein as that adopted by Cream himself in previous letters he had written in an effort to incriminate others, and it would be tempting to ascribe the Vestry Hall exhibit to him also were it not for the fact that he was, prior to his appearance at the inquest, under strict surveillance in Holloway Gaol.

What really excited the coroner and the court – gave them a touch of the Boris Kharlofs, as it were – was that the letter was signed "Yours respectfully, Juan Pollen, *alias* Jack the Ripper." However, if Mr. Pollen's well-meant intervention failed to save Neill Cream from the gallows, its gratuitous testimony that the gravely wronged doctor was not Jack the Ripper was quite superfluous – that little matter was taken care of by the fact that at the material time Cream was serving a prison sentence in the Illinois State Penitentiary, in the United States of America.

No. 6. Prince Albert Victor Christian Edward (Duke of Clarence and Avondale): In 1970 there appeared in *The Criminologist* an article by Dr. Thomas Stowell so thinly veiled that, instead of being captioned *A Solution to the Jack the Ripper Mystery*, it might have been introduced by the lines:

> *When the Duke of Clarence,*
> *Lost his Balance.*

Indeed a couplet would have been most appropriate, for throughout his article Stowell persisted in referring to his suspect as "S", when his allusions and choice of words, oblique and equivocal as they were, made it plain that he meant none other than Queen Victoria's grandson the Duke of Clarence, known to his intimates as Eddy.

Dr. Stowell's evidence was based on the private papers of Sir William Gull, Physician Extraordinary to Queen Victoria, and is so at variance with the facts in small (and not so small) matters that little confidence can be reached in the ultimate conclusion we are expected to draw – that young "collar and cuffs", as Eddy was known, was indeed a Royal Ripper.

Stowell's errors read like a catalogue. For example, he claims that Eddy did not die, as the history books suggest, in the 'flu epidemic of 1892, but of syphilis, information that could not, incidentally, have been culled from the Gull papers, since Sir William himself died in 1890. Stowell also claims that Eddy had to resign his commission in the army, which he did not, and that the Royal Family knew that he was the murderer, if not soon after the first murder then following the second, which if they did must have convinced them of the young man's supra-natural powers as well as of his guilt, for on those dates he was in Scotland on a shooting expedition.

Understandably alarmed at such propensities in a member of the Blood Royal, Eddy, according to Stowell, was then shut up by his family in a private asylum, escaping just long enough to dispose of Mary Kelly at Miller's Court on November 9th. In fact, between the dates of November 3rd and November 12th, Eddy was at Sandringham in connection with his father's birthday celebrations, following which he went to Denmark.

It would be tempting, therefore, to say that Dr. Stowell's article was quite wrong, that the Duke died of pneumonia, following influenza, on January 14th, 1892, aged twenty-eight, and to leave it at that. Unfortunately we can't, for that most provocative of recent writers, Stephen Knight, is there to tell us that in aiming his word-barbed arrows at Eddy, the devious doctor actually meant them to pierce the heavily protected hide of someone quite different.

No. 7. Stephen, James Kenneth: In his particular game of fitting the Ripper's slipper, Michael Harrison, in his book *Clarence*, rejects the Duke and finds his homicidal Cinderella in the person of Clarence's tutor at Cambridge, James Kenneth Stephen. And the motive? A homosexual relationship between the two – possibly no more than platonic – that, diminishing as time passed, and particularly after Clarence was gazetted into the army in the June of 1885, left Stephen in the grip of a perverted sense of loss and grievance that, battening on an already near pathological hatred-cum-fear of women, drove him to commit the Whitechapel atrocities in 1888.

There is no doubt, of course, that following a serious head injury in 1887 – when that part of his anatomy came into contact either with a projection from a passing train or with the rotating vane of a windmill – Stephen became very odd indeed, and that when his protracted periods of inertia lifted he would exhibit all the signs of inspirational mania. He was, in short, going mad, becoming Sir William Gull's patient in 1887, and under whose care he still was when he published two collections of poems.

It is these that, in style and expression, Harrison and others have sought to link with certain of the Ripper letters, and thus with Stephen. One such spasm of Stephen's mordant creativity runs as follows:

> *If all the harm that women have done*
> *Were put in a bundle and rolled into one,*
> *Earth would not hold it,*
> *The sky could not enfold it,*
> *It could not be lighted nor warmed by the sun;*
> *Such masses of evil*
> *Would puzzle the devil*
> *And keep him in fuel while Time's wheels run.*

Clearly, James Kenneth Stephen did not like the ladies, but whether he loathed them – and himself – so much that he degenerated into an albeit uncommon murderer is extremely doubtful.

In 1891, the same year that he wrote his books of verse, Stephen was committed to an asylum where he died in the February of 1892, without, as far as is known, again putting pen to paper. Had he done so, we might have been marginally more, or less, enlightened . . .

> *Time was when I, as Eddy's Tutor,*
> *Enjoyed his love as sage and Suitor,*
> *But as time passed*
> *On passion's last*
> *I spent my urge as Death's Recruiter.*

No. 8. Deeming, Frederick Bayley:

> *On the twenty-third of May,*
> *Frederick Deeming Passed away;*
> *On the scaffold he did say:*
> *"Ta-ra-ra-boom-di-ay !"*
> *"Ta-ra-ra-boom-di-ay !"*
> *An East End holiday,*
> *Jack the Ripper's gone away.*

This is one of the perennial pegs upon which hangs the rumour that Frederick Deeming, the Rainhill, Liverpool, murderer who cemented relations with Australia by using that quick-setting commodity to secure his victims beneath heartstones both there and in England, was also the Whitechapel journeyman.

Following his execution in Australia on May 23rd, 1892, Deemings death mask was sent to Scotland Yard, an unwholesome reminder that its original was regarded in some quarters as being more infamous than even his wife and child-killing exploits allowed. Actually, Frederick Bayley Deeming was otherwise engaged at the relevant time, being in prison in England in connection with something quite different.

A scene from the Whitechapel Road at the turn of the century. By courtesy City of London Guildhall Library.

No. 9. Jill the Ripper: William Stewart, in his book *Jack the Ripper: A New Theory*, really set out to perfect the "invisible man" concept – the postman or policeman type of person whom nobody notices because he is *expected* to be where he is and does not, therefore, excite the observer's curiosity – by changing Jack into Jill, and, furthermore, into that sort of woman who could *. . . pass through the streets in blood-stained clothing without arousing suspicion . . . bring to bear sufficient knowledge to conduct the mutilations . . .* and who could, if challenged at the scene of her crime, give *. . . a plausible explanation of her presence.*

Stewart's solution was *. . . a woman who was or had been a mid-wife, and who might well have been an abortionist,* and it is an appealing facet of his hypothesis that it was just such a person who, having donned Mary Kelly's clothes after killing her inside No. 13 Miller's Court, was seen in the street by Mrs. Caroline Maxwell. This deft touch is, however, spoiled by two things – that Black Mary's clothes were still in her room when the police broke in, and that Mrs. Maxwell claimed to have *spoken* to Kelly that morning.

Jill the Ripper was revived in 1972, when Ex-Detective Chief Superintendent Arthur Butler, writing in *The Sun* newspaper, added his weight and an accomplice to Stewart's contention that the female Ripper was an abortionist.

One of Butler's assertions, which are really models of what a policeman could never expect to say in court without being acutely challenged, presents Jill's partner as a sort of knacker's porter who, for example, trundled Annie Chapman's body – lolling head and all – through the streets in a perambulator.

With a little encouragement Mr. Butler might have been persuaded to put his further thoughts on the subject into rhyme, if not reason:

> *Jack and Jill set out to kill,*
> *And carried out a slaughter,*
> *For half-a-crown,*
> *They went to town,*
> *Then blamed it on their daughter.*

Well, perhaps not; two of them are quite enough, without starting a family.

No. 10. The Ritual Slaughterman: Robin Odell's candidate for the role of Jack the Ripper, as related in his book *Jack the Ripper in Fact and Fiction,* fulfils several of William Stewart's criteria – those of "conditioned invisibility", freedom from suspicion though blood-stained, and having the skill and knowledge to carry out the necessary knife-work. He was, however, not a woman, but a *shochet,* or ritual slaughterman.

There was in Whitechapel in 1888 a Jewish abattoir where such slaughtering and dressing of animals took place, and there were, no doubt, as many *shochets* as were needed to cater for a substantial immigrant population. These *shochets* were important men in the community, being junior clerics of some learning and intellect, and steeped in the teachings and traditions of their faith and calling. In appearance they would be soberly, even somberly, dressed, with the corresponding mien of those in a position of trust.

Having thus gained their confidence, Odell's Jewish *shochet* would certainly have been up to the task of destroying the women' of his choice, for in his legitimate business he was an adept, when performing the *shecita,* at drawing his perfectly honed knife across the throat of an animal, and cutting right back to the bone. He would then conduct his own *post mortem,* involving entry into the great body cavities to check the major organs for any signs of damage or disease. If everything proved satisfactory, the beast was declared *kosher.*

Donald Rumbelow, who is very strong on the likelihood of the Ripper strangling his victims before putting them to the knife, argues that this technique would necessarily rule out the ritual slaughterman, and does not, in any case, agree with Odell that only a *shochet* would have had the professional aptitude to employ the knife so adroitly.

As to the *shochet's* motive and the reason for his moon-lighting activities coming to an abrupt end, Odell packages the two neatly enough when he suggests that his suspect was suffering from a peculiar form of religious mania; that . . . *lurking behind the respected character of the ritual slaughterman was the mind of a sexual sadist* and that his end was encompassed by his own people . . . *who may have dealt with him according to their own brand of justice.*

One thing is certain, if Robin Odell's Jewish ritual slaughterman was guilty of the Ripper murders, his victims were generally so physically as well as morally degenerate that he must have regarded their flesh as *trefah,* unfit or forbidden, rather than *kosher.*

No. 11. Cutbush, Thomas; Kosminski; and Ostrog, Michael: Further reference to the official MacNaghten notes throws but dim light on three more Ripper suspects, as the following extracts indicate . . . *Thomas Cutbush, who was arraigned at the London County Sessions in April 1891, on a charge of maliciously wounding Florence Grace Johnson, and attempting to wound Isabelle Frazer Anderson in Kennington, was found to be insane and sentenced to be detained during Her Majesty's pleasure. This Cutbush . . . escaped from the Lambeth Infirmary (after he had been detained there only a few hours as a lunatic), at noon on 5th March, 1891. He was rearrested on the 9th idem . . . [Cutbush] apparently contracted syphilis about 1888, and since that time, led an idle and useless life. His brain seems to have become affected, and he* *believed that people were trying to poison him . . . He is said to have rambled about at night, returning frequently with his clothes covered with blood, but little reliance could be placed on the statements made by his mother or his aunt, who both appear to have been of a very excitable disposition. It was impossible to ascertain his movements on the nights of the Whitechapel murders. The knife found on him was bought in Houndsditch about a week before he was detained in the Infirmary.*

Harking back to the Druitt reference, MacNaghten goes on . . . *I may mention the cases of three men, any one of whom would have been more likely than Cutbush to have committed this series of murders* . . . He then names Druitt, Kosminski, a Polish Jew, and Michael Ostrog, a Russian doctor. Of Kosminski, MacNaghten writes . . . *This man became insane owing to many years indulgence in solitary vices. He had a great hatred of women, especially of the prostitute class, and had strong homicidal tendencies: he was removed to a lunatic asylum about March 1889. There were many crimes connected with this man which made him a strong suspect.*

And of Michael Ostrog . . . [he] *was frequently detained in a lunatic asylum as a homicidal maniac. This man's antecedents were of the worst possible type, and his whereabouts at the time of the murders could never be ascertained.*

Further examination of the Cutbush episode, following a sensational article in the *Sun* newspaper of February 1894, strongly suggests that Thomas Cutbush was a ripper only in the sense that he went about slashing at women's dresses, and that the knife he used, far from being the dreadful Whitechapel weapon, was, as MacNaghten's notes prove, bought long after the Ripper murders were over and done with.

Of Kosminski and Ostrog what can one say except – *who?* They are both, according to MacNaghten, likely enough prospects yet neither figures "king size" in press or police records, and one is forced to the conclusion that they are part and parcel of the general mix-up involving Klosowski (Chapman) and Pedachenko.

No. 12. Gull, Sir William: Sir William Gull is remarkable in Ripperology in that his credentials as Sir William *Ripper*, alias Sir *Jack* Gull, have been presented in three distinct stages, each gaining substance, if not universal credibility, in the process.

He is first Gul-*libled* as the result of a trance-like experience attributed to the medium R. J. Lees who, it seems, had a series of visions during the first of which he "saw" the Whitechapel Murderer dressed in . . . *a dark tweed suit and a light-coloured overcoat.*

Sometime later, Lees actually spotted the fellow at Shepherd's Bush, but, unable to persuade a policeman that precognition had relinquished its initial letter, he failed to round up his quarry. Eventually, however, more senior officers took him in turn seriously and to a fashionable house of his nomination in the West End.

The doctor who lived there admitted to lapses of memory and to other suspicious circumstances, and the clothes in his wardrobe tallied with those seen in Lees' sartorial seance. The doctor, who wanted to do away with himself when he realised what he had done, was instead examined by a commission of lunacy and placed in an asylum. The questions we have to consider are: was Lees reliable, and if so was the address he and the police visited No. 74 Brook Street? Because if it was, that was where Sir William Gull resided.

For the next installment of the Gull serial we are indebted to more recent times when, in a BBC televison series titled *Jack the Ripper*, later published in book form as *The Ripper File*, the fictional detectives Charlie Barlow and John Watt, put Sir William under the modern microscope.

The primary witness for the police was Joseph Sickert, son of the painter Walter Sickert, who alleged that the murders had been committed by Sir William Gull, assisted by a coachman called John Netley. Sickert's contention was that the Duke of Clarence, he who eddies wanly in and out of the Ripper affair like an air consumptive, had been a regular visitor to an artists' colony in Cleveland Street, and had fallen for a girl known as Ann Elizabeth Crook, or Cook, who worked in a tobacconist's shop nearby, and that these two became secretly married.

That there was a girl-child previous to his clandestine union, that the bride was a common commoner and a Catholic, and that England was known to be riddled with subversive elements was, it was feared, the stuff that caused thrones to totter. All of which prompted the then Prime Minister, Lord Salisbury, to take steps. According to the authors, the steps he took were to have Cleveland Street raided and Clarence's wife committed to Guy's Hospital and, subsequently, to Fulham Hospital, where she died in 1920.

If at this stage one is tempted to ask "So Whatt?" with two t's, the implication of the TV investigation presumably was that, even at this comparatively early stage of a cover-up, Sir William Gull was involved because he was once superintendent of a small lunatic asylum for women at the first of the two hospitals, and could have retained sufficient influence to have Ann Elizabeth incarcerated there.

Having bought that, as the saying goes, it is a short step to ask us to accept that Gull's intervention was at the behest of Lord Salisbury, with the early objective of silencing a witness to that marriage of maximum inconvenience – *Mary Jane Kelly.*

Already Sir William Gull is looming so large that he is no longer Gull but Gulliver, and we are reminded of the Stowell article of 1970 . . . *Gull was seen more than once in Whitechapel on the night of a murder, being there . . . for the express purpose of certifying the murderer insane.*

Who saw him is a more loaded question than might at first sight appear, in that if, as we are given to understand, Stowell was quoting from Gull's own papers, the witness must have been Gull himself! It is, therefore, appropriate that such a boomerang conclusion should introduce the most astonishing Ripper theory so far – that presented in Stephen Knight's *Jack the Ripper: The Final Solution.* In it, Knight's fusion of facts and interpretive ideas constitute a literal *tour-de-force*, for his Ripper is not one man but three, and their activities soon make is plain that the only cover-up they are interested in is the sort that involves a coffin.

What Knight does is to take the *morgue*anatic marriage of the TV Ripperlogue as a starting point and extrapolate its implications to the *n*th degree, exposing in the subsequent cover-up the participation of men in both high and low places, all of them Masons, some of them privy to the purpose of eliminating the threat of blackmail posed by Mary Kelly and the gin-tongued drabs she had confided in, a very few of them party to the drastic means to be adopted.

One man, according to Knight, who embraced every aspect of this Masonic cover-up was General Sir Charles Warren, himself a high-ranking Freemason, who used his position as operational head of the Metropolitan Police to suppress evidence that might in any way point to his fellow Mason Gull. Again according to Knight, this was the motive attaching to Warren's deletion of the reference to *Juwes* – J-U-W-E-S – in Goulston Street, a term applying not to those of the Jewish race but, in Masonic mythology, to the three apprentice Masons *Jubela, Jubelo* and *Jubelum.*

It was Warren too who pigeon-holed much of the statement made by the man Schwartz, following Elizabeth Stride's murder in Berner Street, and who reacted so precipitately to the news that a man had bought Stride grapes at Matthew Packer's shop, lest such information implicated Gull's coachman Netley, and through him Gull and his shadowy companion. The grapes themselves, the significance of which played such an esoteric part in events, created the consternation they did on account of the fact that Sir William Gull was known to be partial to the fruit, and the rumour that poisoned grapes were employed to anaesthetize, if not kill, the Ripper victims.

That Stephen Knight paints a picture in three dimensions, that his research is as meticulous as it is massive, and that he surprises as well as compels is to understate the case, for as well as being a definitive work on the subject, *Jack the Ripper: The Final Solution* is also what pipe-smoking reviewers, with short back and sides, used to call "A rattling good yarn".

Gull's third man, the chap who jogs around with him inside Netley's hearse-like coach, is introduced very early on, and is no less a personage than Sir Robert Anderson, the brand new Assistant Commissioner of the Metropolitan Police who went to Switzerland in search of *edelweiss* straight after the Chapman murder. What we do not anticipate is that towards the end of the book the author ditches the urbane Sir Robert in favour of another.

Whether one can accept this construction and its conclusions is another matter, and one that can only be reached after reading Mr. Knight's book at least as many times as he claims there are Rippers, or, for that matter, Apprentice Masons. For this reader there remains the incongruity of the young and still attractive Kelly making intimates of middle-aged down-starts such as Polly Nichols and Annie Chapman, and of the unholy trio of Gull, Netley and A. N. Other mistaking Kelly for that reduced remnant of humanity Catherine Eddowes. But, then, Stephen Knight has answers for this too.

Epilogue

Rich man, poor man, beggar-man, thief . . .?

SO when all is done and said, the one incontrovertible truth that is known about the identity of Jack the Ripper . . . is that the identity of Jack the Ripper is not known.

What is known is that there was, in the East End of London during that fear-fraught autumn, what many came to regard as an atmosphere of perverted logic that placed reason in a straight-jacket and the Ripper at an advantage, for the police of the day were so socially blinkered that it only required a well-dressed suspect, however compromised, to prove a respectable, i.e., a middle- or upper-class address, to be released *sans* search or further interrogation.

The effect of this policy was for the police to look for the Ripper in the common lodging-houses, among the market and slaughter-house workers, the docks' labourers, and amidst those elements of the feckless and the workless that congregated in Whitechapel like threadbare patches in the fabric of a garment. It would have been a thankless task at the best of times, but hampered as they were by a lack of resources and direction from above, the police of 1888 drew a yawning blank.

It was largely due to this failure that the Ripper acquired the stature he ultimately did, and which caused Matters and most writers since to seek a solution to the riddle in the concrete form of certain solid citizens, rather than among the *hoi polloi*; that and the fact that there is infinitely more compulsion attached to writing and reading about the unacceptable faces of the wealthy and the respected.

And yet all these literary sleuths, like the police before them, have failed to indict a culprit about who it can be said that he and he alone was guilty beyond a shadow of a doubt of the Whitechapel murders; that he and he alone was Jack the Ripper. Instead we are spoilt for choice, and the choice is spoilt by too many loose ends, too many contradictions, and too little appetite for the unpalatable probability that the Ripper was a mere nobody after all; which, if this were so, would at least exonerate the police from failing because they were looking in the wrong place.

In this context, the one thing that emerges above all others is that Jack the Ripper knew every inch of Whitechapel, not in the way that those who went slumming knew it, nor even those like the clergy and the social workers at Toynbee Hall whose vocations took them there, but as surely as the London cab horse knew its way back to the rank and a welcome nose-bag.

The Ripper knew the beats and points of constables, he knew the reticule of streets and passages between Spitalfields market in the west and the Jews

Cemetery in the east as a rabbit knows the labyrinthine burrows of its own warren, he knew unerringly of a public sink set well back from the pavement in Dorset Street, he knew betwixt and between all these places when and where to go to ground; in short, he exhibited all the nous and local knowledge of someone native to or intimate with those parts.

Equally, the Ripper knew how to kill, not necessarily with the finesse of a surgeon, but nevertheless professionally with the swift, strong, capable strokes of a man used to spilling blood and opening up a body, and there is contained in Donald Rumbelow's *The Complete Jack the Ripper* the transcript of a letter, both literate and instructive, received by the police from a qualified butcher who makes out a very strong case for the killer having come from the slaughtering and dressing fraternity.

One passage in particular describes vividly what might have happened to Polly Nichols, and the rest . . . *He would know his work too well to attempt to cut the throat . . . while standing up, but . . . with one hand over the mouth and the thumb under the chin, then with what is known in the trade as a shaking (striking) knife . . . in the twinkling of an eye he has cut the throat, then turning the head to one side, like he would a sheep, the body would bleed out whilst he did the rest of the work. . . .* How true to life (or death) is that about draining the body, for was not the head of each of the Ripper's victims so inclined?

Nor need such a butcher have been following his trade at the time of the murders. Like Rumbelow's man who wrote of being one . . . *From the age of fourteen years till past thirty*, he might have turned to something else. There were, for instance, a good many cattle-boats plying between the East End docks and the Continent, and he could have been working on one of these, a possibility that would account for the timing of each murder at a week-end, the period when such craft were normally lying at the wharfs.

It could also account for the killings ending so abruptly and without explanation, for while a sudden death or committal to an asylum of someone living in the Whitechapel area would no doubt have been related to events and looked into, there need have been no positive association made with a man dying or going stark raving mad on board ship, or on the other side of the Channel.

Only slightly less attractive than a butcher as a suspect, in that he would know how to open up a body and remove vital organs, if not how to kill expeditiously, would be a mortuary attendant. He would have seen surgeons do such things often enough and doubtless done the work himself on occasion; there would, in any case, have been no lack of access to the proper instruments and no need to keep them other than in their rightful place.

But all is conjecture, all is speculation, and if we were to permutate every fact and fancy at our disposal, we should inescapably arrive at the finding with which this epilogue began . . . *that the identity of Jack the Ripper is not known.* What, then, remains to be done? Is it to marshal every scrap of relevant information, to assemble every conceivable suspect, and thus armed to programme the very last thing in micro-chip-brained computers? Perhaps it is. Perhaps in this way we might arrive at the sort of answer given to the question about which is the better watch, one that gains five seconds a day or one that doesn't go? The micro-detectives have a very crisp answer to that: the one that doesn't go, of course; *that* is exactly right twice a day.

Relating this irrefutable logic to the Ripper problem, it might be that by feeding in sufficient suspects, say everybody alive in London between August the 31st and November the 9th, 1888, a computer with a death-wish for terminal indigestion might reveal who *didn't* do it.

Another facet of the Whitechapel Road. It was behind this facade that Jack the Ripper laid siege to the unacceptable face of Victorian London.

BIBLIOGRAPHY

ACKNOWLEDGEMENTS

LIBRARY MAP

OF

LONDON

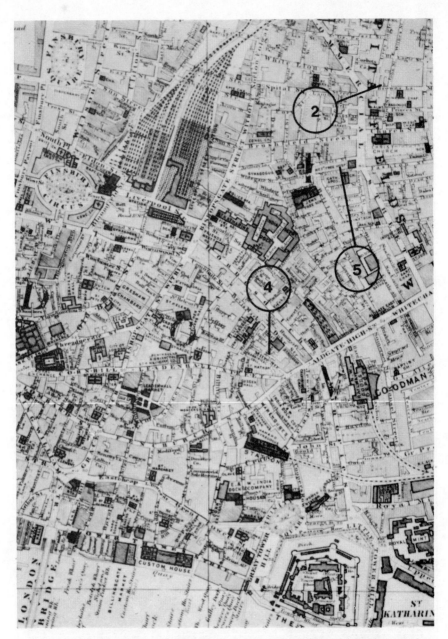

Stanford's Library Map of London & its Suburbs, including the sites of the Ripper Murders of 1888. The map fragments appearing on pages 7, 12, 17, 23 and 36 can be related to

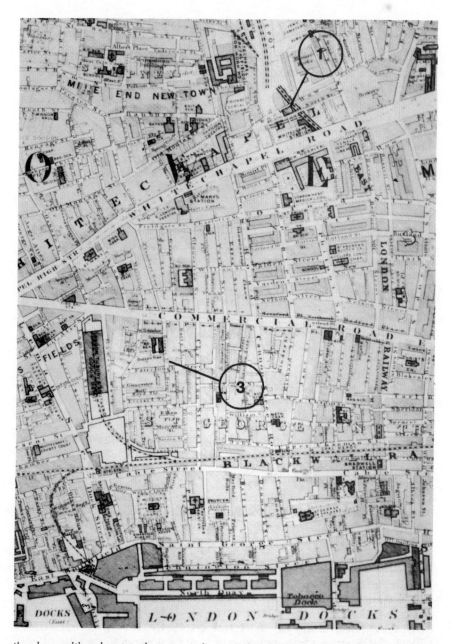

the above, although not to the same scale. Reproduced by arrangement with the City of London Guildhall Library. Please see also note on page 12 concerning Hanbury Street.

Bibliography & Acknowledgements

The following books and sources are referred to in the text of *Will the Real Jack the Ripper*, and constitute required reading for all those who would wish to delve deeper into the minutiae of the Whitechapel murders and the facts and fallacies surrounding them. The present author acknowledges the debt he owes these previous writers and publishers, and in so doing wishes to pay tribute to their contribution to his increasing fascination with and understanding of a compelling subject. Those readers wishing to consult a comprehensive bibliography should acquire *Jack the Ripper: Mysteries of the East End*, *A Bibliography and Review of the Literature*, by Alexander Kelly, published in London by The Association of Assistant Librarians, S.E.D.

Matters, Leonard (W. H. Allen): *The Mystery of Jack the Ripper.*
Odell, Robin (Mayflower-Dell): *Jack the Ripper In Fact and Fiction.*
Cullen, Tom (The Bodley Head, and Fontana/Collins): Originally *Autumn of Terror*, and subsequently *The Crimes and Times of Jack the Ripper.*
Farson, Daniel (Michael Joseph, and Sphere Books): *Jack the Ripper.*
Rumbelow, Donald (W. H. Allen): *The Complete Jack the Ripper.*
Knight, Stephen (George G. Harrap, and Granada Publishing): *Jack the Ripper: The Final Solution.*
McCormick, Donald (Jarrolds, and Long): *The Identity of Jack the Ripper.*
Harrison, Michael (W. H. Allen): *Clarence: The Life of the Duke of Clarence and Avondale.*
Leeson, Albert Edward (Stanley Paul): *Lost London.*
Camps, Francis E. (David & Charles): *Camps on Crime.*
Stewart, William (Quality Press): *Jack the Ripper: A New Theory.*

The cover subject is BLIND MAN'S BUFF, first published in *Punch, or the London Charivari*, in 1888. That on the title page is a sketch of Spitalfields Market, and is reproduced by courtesy of the City of London Guildhall Library.

SPECIALIST BOOKSELLERS dealing in second-hand, factual crime subjects:
Bookshop in Norfolk Road, 13 Norfolk Road, Littlehampton, Sussex.
Grey House Books, 12a Lawrence Street, Chelsea, London SW3 5NE.
J. C. G. Hammond, Crown Point, 33 Waterside, Ely, Cambs. CB7 4AU.
Wildy & Sons Ltd., Lincoln's Inn Archway, Carey Street, London WC2.

Will the Real Jack the Ripper also appears in Cassette form (2 x 45 min sides) and is available at most Music Centres. In case of difficulty, please apply direct to SPEAK EEZEE VOICE PRINTS, division of COUNTRYSIDE PUBLICATIONS LIMITED, SCHOOL LANE, BRINSCALL, Nr. CHORLEY, LANCS, price £3.30 inclusive of V.A.T., postage & packing.